SQUARE METRE
GARDENING
for
CANADA

A.H. Jackson

LONE
PINE

Lone Pine Publishing
2311 – 96 Street
Edmonton, AB T6N 1G3
Canada

Website: www.lonepinepublishing.com

Library and Archives Canada Cataloguing in Publication

Jackson, A. H., 1944-
      Square metre gardening for Canada / A.H. Jackson.

Includes index.
ISBN 978-1-55105-891-7

      1. Square foot gardening--Canada.   2. Small gardens--
Canada.   3. Container gardening--Canada.   I. Title.

SB453.3.C2J437 2013   635.0971   C2012-907639-2

Editorial Director: Nancy Foulds
Project Editor: Sheila Quinlan
Production Manager: Gene Longson
Layout and Production: Alesha Braitenbach
Cover Design: Gerry Dotto

Photos: All photos are by Sandy Weatherall except: Alison29 | Dreamstime.com 92b; Anple | Dreamstime.com 167b; Alesha Braitenbach 122; Tamara Eder 20, 33b, 66, 89a, 112, 124b, 126a&c, 131, 135, 217a; Elliot Engley 78a,b&c, 79; Jen Fafard 24, 26, 27, 113; Derek Fell 22a, 25, 128, 152a&b, 164b, 168b, 178a, 187a&b, 189a, 203b, 207a, 210a, 214, 216b, 217b, 218a; Erika Flatt 219; Food-micro | Dreamstime.com 168a; Saxon Holt 13, 215; Simon Howden | Dreamstime.com 70; iStock 104, 108a, 161; Jebournon | Dreamstime.com 45; Jianghongyan | Dreamstime.com 165; Liz Klose 180, 211; Trina Koscielnuk 74; Suzanne Lewis 118, 119; Janet Loughrey 7, 82, 85, 103, 139a, 206b; Erica Markham 76b; Tim Matheson 15, 32, 36b, 59, 65, 67, 68b, 69, 107, 121b&c, 123, 126b, 127, 186, 213; Kim O'Leary 14, 125b; Allison Penko 11b; Laura Peters 9b, 11a, 19, 37, 50, 55, 64, 76a, 88a, 89b, 91, 93, 108b, 109, 125a, 130, 137a&b, 143b, 153b, 154a, 155a&b, 157a, 163b, 166b, 167a, 169a&b, 170a, 173, 176a&b, 177a&b, 183, 184b, 191a, 193b&c, 197b, 198a, 199b, 200, 202b, 203a, 204, 205, 206a, 207b, 208a&b, 209, 210b, 212b; photos.com 10, 18, 44, 58, 60, 120; Robert Ritchie 124a, 132, 134a; Nanette Samol 9a, 17, 21, 22b, 23, 56, 57a, 61, 62, 63, 73, 80, 90, 116, 117, 129, 136, 138a, 140a&b, 144, 145a&b, 147a&b, 148, 149a, 150, 151a&b, 153a, 154b, 156b, 157b, 158a&b, 159a&b, 160, 163a, 166a, 171, 172a, 174a&b, 175a, 178b, 179b, 181b, 182a&b, 184a, 185, 189b&c, 192, 194a&b, 195, 196, 197a, 198b, 201b, 212a, 216a, 218b; Paul Swanson 75, 81, 88b, 133, 139b, 141, 142, 143a, 156a, 162a&b, 170b, 188, 190, 191b, 199a, 202a; Don Williamson 134b; Cindi Wilson | Dreamstime.com 16; Carol Woo 121a.

Illustration (p. 34): Alison Beck

Maps (p. 31): adapted from Natural Resources Canada

We acknowledge the financial support of the Government of Canada through the Canada Book Fund (CBF) for our publishing activities.

PC: 16

Table of Contents

Introduction

This book is for those people marooned on islands of winter-scorched concrete who long for a personal oasis of nutritional green. How people came to reside in the grit and grime of cities instead of the traditional leafy green tranquility of the countryside is a short story with a long title: World Wars I and II, and Korea. Young men and women left the farms to enlist in those conflicts or to labour in factories to produce war materials. When the dust finally settled in the late 1950s, the family farm had all but disappeared, along with those traditional ties that bound Canadians to the socially nurturing rural life and its cornucopia of wholesome foods. Then came television, the end of family dinners and an era of quickie foods that marked the beginning of concrete island life for most Canadians. Work 9–5, pick up imported food at the supermarket, eat, watch TV, sleep, repeat and hope nothing ever changes, that the system of highways, railroads, cheap gas and California produce remains ever operational.

The rural connection may be gone, but the yearning for a more natural life still exists, and adding a small oasis of culinary green will serve to alleviate city dwellers' feelings of abandonment on a sea of concrete. People need greenery, especially in cities, where it becomes a kind of symbiotic relationship. Any constraints may be overcome with planning and a proper execution of those plans. Taken a step further, the relationship can benefit not only the psyche of city dwellers, but also their physical health, as any number of wholesome fruits and vegetables can be grown in square metre gardens. All it takes is a not-complicated memorandum of requirements, expectations and a bit of planning. Healthy, wholesome, pesticide-free produce can be raised in almost any space, whether in raised beds or containers, and we shall examine every one: backyards, patios, balconies, rooftops, windowsills and walls. Where there is sunshine, fresh fruits and vegetables can be raised, and in quantities that will surprise and delight.

A Short History of Square Metre Gardening

Historically, humankind's success at raising food crops has been constrained by water, weeds, weather, insects and time. The early Egyptians, the great pioneers of getting the most from the least, became expert at floodplain seeding in a manner that provided them a maximum return at harvest, a method that in modern times is called intensive planting. Soil left behind as the annual Nile floodwaters receded was soft, moist and required only that a stick be dragged around helter-skelter before seeds were flipped to the wind by a practiced hand. A good flip man could seed acres but was always constrained by water; the harvest had to be up and out before the desert sun baked his field to a brick—an unfortunate and all-too-common occurrence. Grains, legumes and onion plants were left on their own in those large fields, and only the hardiest and fastest-growing plants survived as runts fell to the wayside or got picked off by the farmer's kids.

Time was an omnipresent constraint for those early Egyptian farmers, and "hurry up and grow" was the all-consuming thought until some was given to extending the available growing time of crops with water scooped from the Nile. What they devised was called a *shaduf*, a lever and bucket device that, when operated continuously, forced water into graded channels in the floodplain fields. When farmers stopped levering, the water stopped coming, so they learned very quickly to reduce levering time by broadcasting seeds into smaller, more compact fields. This innovation was undoubtedly appreciated by

Only the hardiest and fastest-growing onions (above) and legumes (below) survived the farming practices of the ancient Egyptians.

wives pressed into dragging the pointed stick used to chug up ground for seeding, but sons and daughters would be unhappy with compact fields because their sharp eyes and nimble fingers were then needed to provide the Egyptian farmer a modicum of defence against insect predation.

Small-field agriculture worked well until the increased demands of a rising population outstripped the Egyptian farmers' ability to lever the shadufs. "Make more" was a thought, and to find strong backs for increased levering, the pharaohs took to raiding the neighbourhood for slaves. It wasn't long before the demands of an ever-rising population eclipsed even the ability of countless slaves to lever enough shadufs, and thought was given to replacing slaves with cattle. All they needed was

a method to make going around horizontally drive a wheel on the vertical—a gear. Rudimentary and constructed of wood, the gear freed thousands of enslaved shaduf labourers for the more serious task of constructing pyramids. The gear was such a technological marvel that, with only slight modifications, it enabled grain milling and increased irrigation by wind- or water-powered wheels for centuries until steam power became dominant in the 19th century.

How Much Wood Can a Woodchuck Chuck? (Intensive Agriculture in the Early Years)

Increasing populations drove the early Egyptian farmers to bigger fields and then bigger families because many small hands were needed to pick away the bugs, but days are short, and demand soon outstripped supply. Egyptian farmers gave answer to the fabled woodchuck question with a resounding, "Not much, because the bugs eat it faster than our kids can pick them off."

This shortage caused the pharaoh's officials to devote thought to the problem of insect constraints and come up with a solution, a rudimentary pesticide in the form of a chemical fumigant. It was only burning sulphur, and while it did help control insects, it also killed many adolescent bug pickers and aroused fears of poisoned food among the privileged classes, who responded by creating extremely intensive courtyard gardens of vegetables, citrus and medicinal herbs. Immortalized on tomb paintings, these gardens follow the same basic design: a rectangular walled

Pest insects such as weevils drove Egyptian farmers to develop a rudimentary pesticide.

garden filled with an astounding array of fruit trees and vegetable plants surrounding a piped-in water supply contained in a rectangular tiled pond.

However, these small intensive gardens did nothing for Egypt's growing population of citizens and slaves who depended on grain for bread, gruel and beer. To meet these demands, the Egyptians opted for larger fields and a grain storage system to counter large-scale insect predation, especially from the dreaded locusts. Locust plagues occurred every 10 to 15 years, and not a leaf would escape predation except those in the gardens of the privileged classes. The compact size of those gardens permitted slaves to quickly weave and erect a protective covering of papyrus reeds.

The small intensive gardens of the privileged classes (perhaps similar to the one above) could be protected during locust plagues by weaving a covering of papyrus reeds (below).

While early Egypt's privileged classes consumed fresh produce in troubled times, the citizenry and slaves made do with drawing rations from the public granaries. Compact intensive gardening provided food security for the privileged and was a concept adopted by those equally privileged classes of other ancient kingdoms, most notably the Kingdom of Babylon.

The Babylonians, like the early Egyptians, built great stone structures using slave labour, but unlike the Egyptians, they preferred to reside in their monoliths. Today, their crowning achievement, the great palace of King Nebuchadnezzar II and its famed Hanging Gardens, is called one of the Seven Wonders of the Ancient World. When first constructed, the great palace was an uncomfortable island of stone that marooned its royal inhabitants from nature. Amytis, the king's wife, became homesick for the lush greenery of her home in the ancient kingdom of Media. "Fix it," ordered King Nebuchadnezzar, and his engineers devoted much thought to ways of raising water to great heights for the installation of gardens. Historians are not sure how they accomplished this task because no records survive, but they will allow that it was most probably a gear and screw apparatus not unlike the one diagramed by and named for the Greek mathematician Archimedes. To keep soil from eroding off their monoliths, the Babylonian engineers employed stone boxes, a concept that has stayed in use over the centuries and in modern times is called raised bed gardening.

This stone raised bed planted with vegetables calls to mind the Hanging Gardens of Babylon.

Olives were and are to this day an important crop in Mediterranean countries.

Although no traces of the great palace and its Hanging Gardens survive, their glory is well mentioned in the writings of the ancient Greeks and Romans. And although modern-day renderings of the Hanging Gardens portray it as a pleasure garden, it was more likely an intensively planted food factory that provided palace inhabitants with a supply of fresh produce and food security.

The early Romans took to intensive agriculture in a big way because they had hungry and restless armies to feed. They piped water, moved and amended soil, developed new pesticides and provided slaves with bamboo poles to deter crop predation by birds, especially in the vineyards. A day without wine was truly a day without sunshine for the Romans, and wine was best enjoyed with bread dipped in olive oil or fish oil, with a side of millet gruel or stewed

lovage and a bit of fish or fowl. The privileged classes fared well, as their large villas in the paved-over metropolis of Rome provided them space for rooftop and courtyard gardens, an emulation of the Babylonian hanging box gardens. Readers lucky enough to have visited a traditional Italian home with a vine-draped patio will easily visualize those early courtyards and rooftop gardens that employed the historical techniques of intensive gardening.

Asians, especially the Chinese, have practiced intensive agriculture from time immemorial, especially with rice. Growing rice is very labour intensive. The rice paddies, or large box gardens, were first ploughed, then flooded and flattened to prevent water runoff. Rice shoots were then planted using the tried and true spacing method of the width of an open hand, as Chinese farmers knew

Squash was one of the "three sisters" in the intensive agriculture system used by some North American First Nations.

exactly how many plants would yield a maximum return. This planting method is still used today with little change, except in non-Asian countries such as the U.S., where aircraft broadcast seeds onto flooded and flattened box-like fields according to wind speed and direction, a modern-day version of hand flipping seeds.

In North America, some First Nations employed a system of intensive agriculture that historians call "the three sisters." The natives constructed mounds, wall-less raised beds if you will, whereon were planted corn, beans and squash, along with a fish head for nutrients. After the corn sprouted, the runner beans would use the corn's stalk for a climbing support; beans also naturally fix nitrogen, a major plant nutrient, in the soil, which benefited the corn and squash. Big-leafed squash would shade the soil and reduce weeds and water evaporation.

In Europe, the privileged classes constructed huge castles with a constant water supply and intensively planted walled gardens, a practice that continued when castles gave way to smaller chateaus and manor houses. At the same time, the lower classes became very adept at intensive farming, and over time, large areas of Britain, France and the Low Countries were checkerboarded with small, compact fields. Woodchucks can chuck only so much wood, and European farmers knew all about time constraints and kept their fields a manageable size, fencing them in with rocks, protective windbreaks or hedgerows. From year to year, European farmers knew what to expect from their compact fields and what was required in the way of nutrients.

A few farmers became so expert at crop management that they were hired by local gentry to tend their walled kitchen gardens, and a new profession was born: gardener. Professional gardening was quickly divided into landscape and kitchen gardening, with the latter responsible for a new invention called a conservatory or greenhouse, a heated raised-bed structure with a glass canopy that allowed for year-round planting. Both kitchen gardens and conservatories are historical icons of intensive gardening. Every square metre was expected to provide for the master of the house, and for his weekend guests, who sometimes numbered in the hundreds. English kitchen gardens also supplied the manor house with aromatic flowers for much-needed deodorizing, and in that process they discovered that some flower species, such as sweet alyssum, attract predator insects that feed on common pesky garden bugs. Like the First Nations of North America, they had discovered the benefits of companion planting, and the practice continues into modern times.

Over time and geography, farmers and gardeners inevitably came to the same conclusion: keep it manageable, make sure the soil is sweet and know exactly how many plants will provide maximum yield and at the same time keep down weeds and other pests. That was the game, and since it had no name, we'll call it square metre gardening.

The private greenhouse was a European invention that allowed for year-round planting.

Woodchucks Get Tossed from the Equation

The plow is one of those implements that escaped innovative thought for centuries. A wooden stick with handles it was, and a wooden stick with handles it remained until one fateful morning in 1740 when Robert Ransom, an iron monger from Ipswich, England, jumped out of bed with an idea to cast a plowshare from iron. Not that his invention had much immediate effect on the existing agricultural scene, as fields were small, compact affairs subject to the constraints of labour and representative of how much wood (produce) a woodchuck (farmer) could chuck (plant, grow and harvest).

Improvements to the plow led to larger and larger fields of wheat and rye in France.

However, the French were quick to adopt Ransom's iron plowshare. Ignoring traditional constraints, they cleared vast fields for the monoculture production of wheat and rye grains to make bread for that nation's ever-expanding urban population. Over the years, as they cleared more forests and planted larger fields of grain, their flaunting of those constraints caught up to them. There is a fungus of the family Clavicipitaceae that infects all grass crops including wheat and rye, and it has among its 50 or so family members a pathogen called *Claviceps purpurea*, or ergot, from which the hallucinogen LSD was first synthesized. Ergot has an affinity for rye grain, and in French large-field monoculture it found paradise.

In 1789, the population of Paris rose up and stormed the Bastille, the most fortified structure in the city. It was an act of pure lunacy, and many historians attribute the cause to mass hallucinations caused by consuming bread made with ergot-contaminated rye. The lunacy progressed into a full-scale revolution that featured many months of head loppings and carnival-like executions of royalty until clearer minds began to suspect ergotism and stopped the use of rye grain in bread production. Almost the entire nation had tripped on lysergic acid, a major component of both ergot and synthesized LSD. It was a surreal, macabre bit of history celebrated today as Bastille Day.

In the aftermath of that grotesque occasion all French grains became suspect, resulting in a return to compact grain fields with pathways to allow for government crop inspections. In 1890, Parisian experimental gardeners took compact to the extreme by layering a 2-acre plot 45 cm deep with aged horse manure and placing seeds so close together that, when they matured, formed an indefinable mass that refused weeds even a flicker of sunlight. This experiment was deemed a great success, and after refinements, such as the double digging of manure with soil, it was named French Intensive Agriculture and became the basis of all organic gardening.

The Driving Force of Change

North America, with its previously unimaginable vistas of arable land, would become the driving force behind inventions that pushed agriculture constraints to the horizon: the steel plowshare, mechanical reaper, tractor, seed drill, new pesticides, cheap fertilizers, innovative irrigation, genetically modified plants, and railroads to haul out production. Agriculture switched gears from compact and manageable to an "as far as the eye can see" system of monoculture, with the steel plow and mechanical reaper leading the parade.

Invented by John Deere in 1837, the steel plowshare was a huge improvement

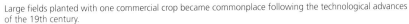
Large fields planted with one commercial crop became commonplace following the technological advances of the 19th century.

over standard iron because it cut soil cleanly and was self-polishing, which freed farmers from interminable stops to unclog the blades. The mechanical reaper, perfected by Cyrus McCormick during the 1830s, enabled a grain farmer to harvest 40 acres a day rather than the previous limit of two or three. Pulling a series of John Deere plows behind large teams of mules or horses turned farmers away from compact, intensive hand-seeded fields to furrowing, meaning they slit and turned ground, drilled and covered seeds in two easy operations and in straight rows. The practice expanded almost to infinity after the introduction of the gasoline-powered farm tractor during the early 1900s.

So much plowing with absolutely no consideration given to constraints would cause a system blow-out in the 1930s, when furrow-plowed prairie lands just dried up and blew away. Known as the Great Dustbowl, it

slammed the brakes on gang-plowing tractors and gave rise to agricultural education and a good hard look at wasteful farming practices, such as the application of fertilizers onto entire fields, which resulted in well-nourished weeds as well as crops, and the exhaustion of soil by repeated planting of identical crops.

Modern farmers are wise to agricultural constraints and are big on crop rotation and fallowing, and while most still broadcast fertilizer over entire fields, the intensive drilling of crop seed counters fertilizer wastage and provides no surface disruption for weeds—the tractors move in straight lines, but when the crop is up the rows are invisible. Nowadays, even corn, that most traditional of row crops, is being planted using no-till methods to husband surface moisture and avoid irrigation. Corn farmers have even taken to skip-row planting, which places corn plants equidistant from one other, enabling an

Poor farming practices were in part responsible for the Great Dustbowl of the 1930s.

even uptake of surface moisture during the all-important initial growing stage.

Modern-day farmers have wised up to agricultural constraints, but many home gardeners are still stuck in the past. Most people with the space still buzz their large plots with a Rototiller, plant long rows with wide aisles and use too much pesticide, fertilizer and sweat. It is time for Canadian gardeners to take a page from history and return to the small raised bed method of growing produce. It is the better way, and by following a few simple rules the Canadian gardener, regardless of available space, can greatly reduce dependence on factory-farmed and imported produce and never have to worry about accumulated pesticide residues, salmonella infections or the long-term effects of consuming genetically modified (GMO) foods.

Modern-day corn farmers use various techniques to conserve moisture in the soil.

What is Wrong with Commercial Produce?

Most of the fruits and vegetables in the produce sections of grocery stores have been imported from another country. Much of it comes from the United States, but Canada also imports produce from as far away as South America and Asia, whose countries have different agricultural standards than do the U.S. and Canada. And though it may look yummy, looks can be deceiving. Even local factory-farmed produce is not always the best quality.

Commercial produce may look good, but looks can be deceiving.

Nutrient-depleted Soils

That an exclusive diet of hamburgers, hot dogs and fries will cause human diseases is common knowledge. Then why is it so difficult for Canadians to realize that a diet restricted to fertilizers containing only three nutrients—nitrogen, phosphorus and potassium (NPK)—could be a cause for disease in plants?

Soil bolstered with commercial NPK fertilizers containing only three of the more than 50 macro- and micronutrients required for optimal plant growth produce food crops lacking life-sustaining nutrients, the ability to resist diseases and weed infestation, and taste. To counter insect and weed infestations, North American factory farmers rely on an arsenal of permitted pesticides. The various categories of pesticides include insecticides, herbicides, rodenticides and fungicides, and farmers apply around one billion kilograms of these poisons annually. As if to add insult to injury, the factory farms, and let's not forget the conglomerate livestock operations, are dumping this humungous amount of poison onto crop plants that bioscientists jokingly call Frankensteins, the genetically modified plants with a built-in ability to withstand applications of more concentrated poisons.

Accumulated Pesticides

An astounding 700 million kilograms of pesticides are applied to food crops in North America, with another 300 million applied by ranchers, poultry farmers, produce shippers and home gardeners, making a nice round figure of 1 billion kilograms annually. In Canada, the tons of pesticides dumped, pumped and sprayed into the environment have formed a pervasive and persistent national dust that is found almost everywhere, especially in our food and water.

Unless it rains, sunshine dissipates most pesticides, and factory farms do not apply pesticides when rain threatens or during crop irrigation. But into every life a little rain must fall, and when it catches factory farmers by surprise it costs them big, as pesticides are expensive and a runoff requires reapplication. The initial application dissolves into the rainwater, soaks into the soil and is taken up by thirsty crops. It's hit or miss, but common sense dictates caution when purchasing produce because that Frankenstein lettuce in the supermarket may contain more poison than Snow White's apple.

As bad as that sounds, it gets worse. Offshore factory farms are seldom constrained by pesticide permits, and their arsenal often includes extremely toxic poisons not permitted for use in Canada; yet their produce easily makes its way to our supermarkets.

During winter, Canadian consumers of foreign produce come into contact with pesticide residues simply by picking up and examining fruits and vegetables.

Nectarines are one of the worst fruits for pesticide residues.

Produce with the Least Pesticide Residue

- Asparagus
- Avocados
- Bananas
- Beans
- Broccoli
- Cabbage
- Cantaloupe (U.S. or Canadian)
- Cauliflower
- Cilantro
- Corn, sweet
- Cranberries
- Grapefruit
- Kiwi
- Mango
- Mushrooms
- Onions
- Papaya
- Peas
- Pineapple
- Tangerines
- Watermelon (U.S. or Canadian)

Produce with the Most Pesticide Residue

- Apples*
- Celery*
- Cherries
- Grapes (imported)
- Kale
- Lettuce
- Peaches and nectarines*
- Pears
- Peppers, hot (imported)
- Peppers, bell
- Potatoes
- Spinach
- Strawberries
- Watermelon (imported)

*Around 95 percent of apples, celery, peaches and nectarines continually test positive for high levels of dozens of pesticides.

The natural wax coating on plums is much different than the food-grade wax applied to commercial produce before shipment.

Waxy Produce

Much of Canada's imported and factory-farmed produce is coated with food-grade wax, which not only protects produce from dehydration and bruising but also provides a shiny, fresh-looking surface. Because most produce has a natural wax coating removed during washing, the rationale is that it is okay to apply a substitute coating. The problem is, many foreign shippers use paraffin wax derived from used oil that may contain toxic elements, such as heavy metals. They also add mould inhibitors to the wax, such as calcium propionate and other chemicals. Consumers of non-organic fruits and vegetables are advised to peel or scrub the produce with a sponge dipped in white vinegar or baking soda, or use a commercial vegetable wash.

Sewage Sludge

Both the U.S. and Canada prohibit the use of untreated and semi-treated sewage sludge for agricultural purposes due to contamination by heavy metals, drugs and PCBs. However, if the product is renamed biosolids, farmers have no problem acquiring this dangerous material. Offshore agricultural production is unrestrained by such prohibitive mandates, and the use of cheap sewage sludge, which may contain human pathogens and heavy metals, as fertilizer has become increasingly popular, further endangering consumers.

The Failing Health of Canadians

Pesticides and nutritionally deficient foods are causing health problems for Canadians. It's up to us to start making good food choices and return to healthy living.

Pesticide-related Health Problems

Every time we look, we're finding out these pesticides are more dangerous than we ever thought before and more toxic at lower levels.

–Phillipe Grandjean, professor, Harvard University School of Public Health

The story of Snow White and the Seven Dwarfs was a bedtime story told to Eastern European children long before the Brothers Grimm wrote down their version in 1812. In the ancient version, Snow White was put to sleep by a poisoned ring; the Brothers Grimm creatively changed it to an apple, as people of that time were beginning to suspect that the lead hydrogen arsenate used to spray apple trees was somehow migrating into the fruit, causing what had become an epidemic of stomach cancer.

This public assumption of poisoned apples by Europeans proved correct; after the pesticide was banned, stomach cancer quickly became a medical rarity. However, the use of lead arsenate continued in Southern Ontario's apple orchards until 1976 and is still used by many overseas growers. Consumers of apple juice are advised to check the product source, as Canadian juice packers are prone to using apple concentrates

It's thought that pesticide-poisoned apples were responsible for an epidemic of stomach cancer in 19th-century Europe. The pesticide is still in use today in some parts of the world.

Even pyrethrin-based pesticides, derived from certain flowers, are no longer considered safe.

from China and Argentina that are likely to contain high levels of lead arsenate along with other pesticide residues.

Pesticides are still causing all manner of health problems including cancers, asthma, reproductive problems and birth defects. In 1985, over 1000 people in the U.S. and Canada were poisoned by imported watermelons grown in soil treated with Aldicarb, a systemic insecticide used to control a wide variety of insects. Aldicarb is a carbamate insecticide and a main ingredient in nerve gas, and though not used in Canada since 1969, the chemical is so pervasive that residues still remain in water aquifers, streams and lakes. It's nasty stuff, and it's all over imported produce, especially potatoes because it is used to control nematodes in soil.

Pyrethrin-based insecticides made from chrysanthemum flowers and long touted as being safe have in fact been responsible for the majority of adverse pesticide-related health reports over the last decade. These are the brand-name household and garden sprays used with wild abandon by almost all Canadians. These products are dangerous and should be used sparingly. Exposure to retailed pesticides has been proven to lower intelligence and cause permanent brain damage in children.

Chlorpyrifos, a potent organophosphate pesticide related to nerve gasses developed by the Nazis, can be found in well water, aquifers and the Great Lakes, with the highest concentrations found in Lake Ontario. Chlorpyrifos is suspected of causing a variety of cancers and was banned in the U.S. in 2000, but it is still being used by Canadian conglomerate farmers and government agencies for aerial mosquito eradication programs. That most Canadians drink this stuff on a daily basis is cause for concern because the long-term effects

Bouquets of imported flowers often test positive for dangerous pesticide residues.

are still in question, as are the long-term effects of glyphosate, the active ingredient in the popular herbicide RoundUp.

Atrazine is another herbicide commonly found in Canadian drinking water that has received some press coverage for the growth abnormalities it causes in fish and amphibians.

Canadian conglomerate dairies have for the last few years been cheating the supply management system by importing a mix of milk powder and sugar called "modified milk ingredients," a product originally designed for confectioners but widely adopted as a dairy ingredient. The milk powder used in modified milk ingredients is cause for concern because, depending on where it came from, it may contain large amounts of pesticides, antibacterial agents and hormone residues.

Even sending a loved one a bouquet of flowers can be dangerous for the recipient because flowers from exporting countries such as Colombia, Ecuador, China and India are constantly doused with the extremely toxic, cancer-causing pesticides Malathion, Sevin and chlordane.

Falling Life Expectancy

As for butter versus margarines, I trust cows more than chemists.

—Joan Gussow, author

Bad food choices are shortening the life expectancy of Canadians; 30 percent of the population is clinically obese, type 2 diabetes is epidemic, heart disease kills one in three Canadians, cancer is rampant and billions of tax dollars are spent for care, treatment and the search for cures. We can do our best to stay healthy by eating wholesome fresh foods, drinking pure water, not smoking and getting plenty of exercise. Scientists call it homeostasis, the human body's ability to maintain dynamic equilibrium and throw off disease by way of a healthy immune system.

You are what you eat, and over 65 percent of Canadians consume supermarket produce that has travelled thousands of kilometres and lost half its nutrient value. Not that it had much to begin with. Imported, single-crop vegetable produce—lettuce, radishes, onions, carrots, etc.—is repeatedly grown in nutrient-depleted soils with chemical fertilizers that contain only three (nitrogen, phosphorus and potassium) of the more than 50 macro- and micronutrients plants require for optimum health. Imported produce also likely contains pesticide residues.

As if to add insult to this national injury, Canadians annually spend billions of dollars at restaurants, with most going for doughnuts, pizza and fried foods. These food products contain trans fats, excessive salt, badly processed carbohydrates, preserving chemicals and refined sugars proven to cause disease and shorten life expectancy. Conglomerate food processors further cut into life expectancy with corn sugar, baker's fog bread made from high-gluten, GMO wheat flour, oily foods, nitrite-laced meats and a litany of artificial colours, flavours and chemical additives.

Imported produce, carrots included, is consistently nutrient deprived.

Community gardens are a great way for urbanites short on space to grow their own produce.

The Solution

It's a grim situation, but for Canadian consumers wanting a return to healthy living, the fix is relatively simple: stop buying food from accountants, lawyers and chemists and look to organic farmers and backyard, balcony and rooftop gardens. The home growing of healthy produce is fast becoming a popular endeavour nation-wide, even for those citizens lacking arable space. Community gardens are popping up by the dozens in every major city across Canada. Some of these community gardens contain hundreds of individual allotments; for perspective, Montreal's 76 community gardens provide allotments for 1.5 percent of the city's adult population. Unfortunately, in most Canadian cities, demand for garden allotments outstrips supply and there are long waiting lists. Community gardens are cost effective, provide users with healthy, pesticide-free produce and are great for socializing, as some of the nicest and most interesting people can be found in those gardens.

Long waiting times for community garden allotments have spawned the SPIN garden movement in some cities, with companies arranging for impatient gardeners to borrow arable land in backyards. SPIN stands for "small plot intensive," which is nothing more than square metre gardening in other people's backyards. It is a financial benefit for both gardener and owner because they share the produce. Market prices for imported fresh produce are rising almost daily, and urban farming has become a profitable and healthy endeavour for many Canadians.

Getting Started

Gardens are not made by singing 'Oh, how beautiful,' and sitting in the shade.

–Rudyard Kipling, author

The square metre gardener will need fields to plant in, and for those we must look to the Babylonians, who employed stone boxes to keep their valuable soil from running away, and to the Iroquois, who knew the right plant combinations for maximum yields. Combining the best gardening practices of both cultures will supply modern gardeners with a cornucopia of the freshest, most nutritious produce on the planet.

It is called "square metre gardening" because the ideal field for growing this cornucopia of produce is a raised bed 2.4 m by 1.2 m (8 feet by 4 feet), for an

Whether their raised beds are shallow or deep, constructed of wood or stone, square metre gardeners must fill them with the finest soil.

area of 3 square metres, filled with the finest soil available. Whatever frame the gardener chooses is fine. Several garden gurus have written books that obsess on the boxes or frames and treat soil as incidental or promote the concocting of artificial soils. Supplied with nutrients, plants will grow in almost any medium—a fact long exploited by corporate farming interests who raise crops in worn-out, nutrient-depleted soil by forcing them with fertilizer. I advocate healthy soil for healthy produce.

Knowing Your Climate

Weather means more when you have a garden. There's nothing like listening to a shower and thinking how it is soaking in around your green beans.

–Marcelene Cox, humourist

Before you plant, you must know your climate. Long-time residents will be conditioned to expect late and early frosts, summer heat waves, droughts, deluges and the odd snowfall in May. Still, there are certain things to keep in mind, including hardiness zones and microclimates. Forewarned is forearmed and enables a defence against Mother Nature's weather surprises.

Hardiness Zones and Frost Dates

The Canadian government publishes a Hardiness Zone Map for the entire nation. The country is divided into zones numbered 0 to 8, with 0 designating areas with the roughest, most brutal winters and 8 the mildest. Each number is subdivided by a lower case letter designating slight ameliorations for microclimate, snow cover, wind speed and moisture. Knowing your hardiness zone is important, especially if you are going to be purchasing trees and shrubs or other perennials. However, the map is of little interest to square metre gardeners, who grow mostly annuals, unless they are new to Canada. Square metre gardeners will find frost date information for their area useful: the last frost date in spring, the first frost date in fall, and the average number of frost-free days every year. The square metre gardener's secret weapon to extending the growing season is the garden cloche (see Cloches and Hoop Tunnels, p. 104).

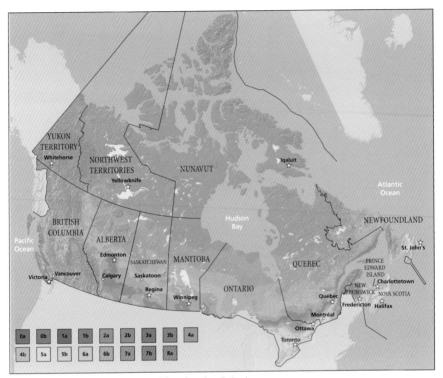

Hardiness zones (above); average annual frost free days (below)

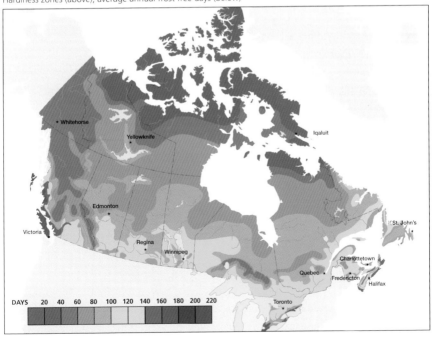

Most Canadians live near large bodies of water, which have an effect on the climate.

Lateral Zones

These zones are not official, but they are as apparent to Canadian gardeners as red noses in winter. Most Canadians reside within 100 miles of the U.S. border, and except for those in the Prairie Provinces, most also live near large bodies of water: the Pacific and Atlantic oceans, and the Great Lakes. Water cools in summer and warms in winter, with big water being superior to small lakes that freeze over early in winter and cease their warming effect.

Microclimates

A few Canadians reside in protected areas, or microclimates, such as a valley on the south side of a mountain range, a prairie land valley, an area near a body of water, or a wind-breaking forest. Square metre gardeners on the rougher end of the scale can ameliorate climate by constructing raised beds close to fencing, shrubbery or buildings, as long as the shelter does not add too much shade to your garden space. Always keep in mind that more sunshine produces more and better produce, so follow your sunshine map (see p. 34) and reserve your areas of maximum sunshine for vegetable plants that will benefit most (see What, When and How Many Seeds, p. 70). Reflective surfaces of buildings can be both curse and blessing as the added heat can help with

Fences can create warmer, more sheltered microclimates in a backyard.

early spring seeding, but it may cause plants to bolt or wilt during a midsummer heat wave. Gardeners may counter too much reflective heat from buildings by draping greenhouse shade cloth over cloches, thereby turning this microclimate into a continual blessing.

Some gardeners residing in extreme low-digit areas have become expert at creating microclimates, and with long periods of daylight are able to produce humungous vegetables, especially cabbage. If a trip to the Yukon is in your future, be prepared for lots of cabbage rolls.

Climate Change

The world is warming up, and not too far into the future, some countries will suffer drastic changes in weather patterns. Countries with previously predictable seasonal rains may come up short, while others in dry desert areas may experience deluge, but a few may actually benefit from climate change.

Canada is one of those few, because in a land of ice and snow any heat is good heat, especially if it allows for a longer growing season. That is happening now, and it's a boon for square metre gardeners, especially those living in southerly areas where cloched (covered) raised beds can be worked almost year-round. Nature gives and takes, and while global warming may give Canadian gardeners a longer growing season and more produce, there will be a marked increase in the numbers and species of insects wanting to take it away, so better be ready for them.

Canadians are used to long, cold winters, but a global warming trend may offer some relief—at a cost.

Mapping Sun, Shade and Growing Space

In addition to knowing your climate, a sunshine map specific to your garden will be an invaluable tool. Knowing where the sun is means knowing where the plants should be.

Most vegetable plants require six to eight hours of sunshine, with six considered "minimum full sun" and eight a paradise for all but leafy vegetables. This requirement is non-negotiable for most vegetable plants and will dictate the placing and size of raised beds and containers. Partial shade is four to six hours of sunshine. It is beneficial for leafy vegetable plants such as lettuce, kale and arugula and is tolerated by certain root vegetables such as carrots and beets. Deep shade, or the dappled shade found under tree canopies, is useless for growing vegetables and should be avoided. Placing beds close to a white fence or garage will give gardeners a head start to the growing season because the sun's reflection off the white surface will raise soil temperatures, but later in the season that same reflection may require some ameliorating in the form of extra watering and shade cloth.

Simply draw a map of your space (scale is not too important) including trees,

Creating a sunshine map will enable more efficient garden planning.

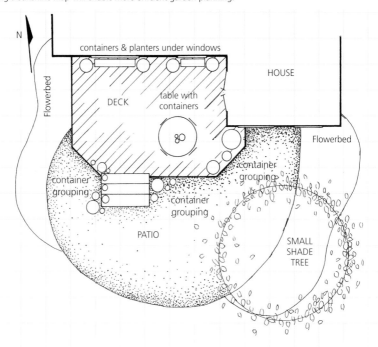

shrubs and fencing, then find five coloured pencils and wait for a sunny day. At 9:00 AM on the sunny day, grab the map and one coloured pencil and go out and observe the space. Draw in areas of sunshine with dotted lines. Repeat every two hours with a different coloured pencil. Map sunshine wherever you find it; if it's on a fence, map and time it, and the same for walls. Vertical spaces are especially important for gardeners on balconies or in other tiny spaces. By 5:00 PM, when the sun begins dropping over the yardarm, it will have left its footprints all over your map. Areas dotted with four or five colours are full sun and a gardener's delight, while areas with three colours are partial shade. It sounds easy and it is, fun too, and also profitable; every square metre bathed in sunshine is money in the pocket and will pay big dividends during harvest time.

Do not hurry this sunshine map; take your time and get it right. Gardeners planning ahead during winter should keep tree and shrub foliage and the changing angle of the sun in mind. Sunshine angles will shift slightly with the changing seasons, but not enough to raise concerns.

The Prognosis

By studying their sunshine map, square metre gardeners are able to ascertain what vessels, how big and how many, will be required to contain soil, and can

Take advantage of sunny wall space; lots of plants like to grow up.

Small areas of sunshine on balconies are perfect for growing herbs.

then draw them onto their sunshine map. Gardeners with substantial space will draw rectangles onto areas of full sun to indicate as many 1.2 m by 2.4 m, or 3-square-metre, raised beds as the space allows. Rectangles that protrude into areas of partial shade are advantageous for growing leafy or baby produce. Small areas of sunshine near back doors, on balconies or on fire escapes, are perfect for growing kitchen herbs or container-crop plants such as tomatoes, and these areas should be marked and measured for vessel requirements. Not to be overlooked are walls and fences that receive over six hours of sunshine, because where there is sunshine there can be vegetables and/or fruits.

Essential Tools

Besides the standard array of garden tools—gloves, a garden fork for the annual turning in of aged manure and compost, a spade for moving and levelling, shears for pruning and harvesting, twine for tying up climbers, a kid's wagon or small wheelbarrow for transporting tools and plants, a shrub rake for tidying and a decent hose and spray nozzle (if not using drip irrigation)—the most essential tool will be the probe thermometer. Inexpensive and available at most garden centres, the probe thermometer allows the square metre gardener to ascertain when soil has reached optimum temperatures for germinating vegetable seeds.

A probe thermometer will be an invaluable tool.

The Soil Vessels

Calling them "soil vessels" sounds almost biblical, and it should. People wanting flowers and fresh produce have been using soil vessels to contain precious soil since time immemorial.

Raised Beds

For gardeners with the space, raised beds are ideal. They can be shallow or deep, and built to fit the yard. I advocate a planting area of 3 square metres as large enough to be prolific, but small enough to be manageable.

The advantages of gardening in raised beds are both varied and numerous. Even if you have the ground space for a standard row garden, the soil is not always great quality. Raised beds can be built to make use of unsuitable ground,

Whether a container or a raised bed, any vessel capable of holding soil is capable of growing plants.

such as wet, rocky or clay areas, and they are aesthetically more pleasing to the eye than traditional in-ground gardens.

In raised beds, the gardener controls the soil quality. And because it is contained, the soil is stable and will not blow away or run off with rainwater. Raised beds are (usually) built small enough that the gardener can reach the centre without having to step on the soil surface, and no stepping on it means no compaction of soil and increased root growth. Better soil aeration means more efficient uptake of nutrients by plants.

Soil in raised beds warms quicker and stays warm longer than in the ground, enabling an earlier and longer growing season. Cloches, or other translucent coverings, may be easily installed to enable even earlier planting. Netting is easily installed to foil bugs, weeds and birds. Even without netting, weeds have little chance in properly planted raised beds.

If space is available, raised beds are ideal for growing vegetables.

Quality, pesticide-free soil enables production of healthier, more nutritious produce with far less disease, such as blossom end rot in tomatoes. The vegetables will also be tastier. Intensive growing means vastly increased vegetable and fruit yields in far less space, allowing for multiple harvests of different vegetables from the same bed.

In the long run, gardeners who grow their vegetables in raised beds rather than buying them at the supermarket will save a small fortune on their grocery bill. They will also save time. A trip to the backyard beats a trip to the market hands down.

Constructing Raised Beds

Think of the aesthetics when constructing raised beds in a backyard. Well-constructed beds will add value to property, especially if the aisles between beds are set with pavers. If you find yourself having to move, it is much easier to sell a home that includes a supermarket produce section in the backyard. And if you're staying put, you'll be able to enjoy the fruits of your labour in a beautiful backyard. Surfing the internet will provide growers with hundreds of design ideas.

Outside of the aesthetics, gardeners should not be overly concerned with raised bed construction; it is simply a vessel to hold and avoid compaction of what is really important to both gardeners and vegetable plants: the soil. Gardeners may employ all manner of materials to construct raised beds— old wood, new wood, cement pavers, stones, bricks, etc. Raised beds can be any length, but 1.2 m (4 feet) is the ideal width, as it permits reaching into the

Well-constructed raised beds will add aesthetic appeal to any backyard.

Brick makes a sturdy, aesthetically pleasing raised bed frame.

centre of the bed without stepping on and compacting the soil. Gardeners with adequate space could install a rectangle of raised vegetable beds with the centre used for seating, along with a perimeter of flower beds for aesthetic value.

Frames for raised gardens may be purchased in kit form, but they are so easily constructed that they can be put together by almost anyone. You will find lots of different raised bed designs online, but the two I've included have been author tested and are probably the easiest way to go. They are basically a child's sandbox to hold quality soil rather than sand. Cedar and redwood are the best lumbers for their construction because they resist rot over time, but almost any untreated lumber will do. For a long-lasting, quality frame, use lumber that will last—cedar, redwood or Douglas-fir—and put it together with screws rather than nails. For gardeners wishing to pursue the aesthetics and be more like the Babylonians, there is stone, brick or pavers. Do not use old railroad ties; they contain creosote or other toxic preservatives.

Reinforce the sides of deep raised beds to keep them from bulging from the weight of the soil inside.

Any material that will hold at least 30 cm of soil above ground level and prevent it from running away is a raised bed frame. The longitudinal dimension of frames is up to the gardener and the sunshine map. But remember, unless you are a basketball player, don't build wider than 1.2 m, as reaching the middle without stepping into the bed and compacting soil is the name of the game. Ideally, the raised bed should be 1.2 m by 2.4 m, for 3 square metres—after all, the process is called square metre gardening.

Beds can be any height, from the standard 30 cm shallow bed up to a maximum of 1.2 m deep for fruit trees; 60 cm is considered an ideal depth for Canadian gardeners because the soil warms quickly in spring and holds heat longer into the autumn months, and it is deep enough for any root vegetable. Keep in mind that higher beds must be adequately reinforced with inside or outside stakes secured to the frame with screws or pipe clamps to prevent boards bulging from the weight of the soil. And more height means more soil, which means more labour to transport it to the beds. However, for elderly gardeners or those with back problems who find bending over difficult, higher frames, perhaps with a mitered cap for sitting, can make gardening easier.

Some garden experts recommend a 90 cm space between beds, claiming

Raised bed aisles need only be wide enough to pull a small wagon through.

mature plants will overflow and restrict space, but I find that amount a bit excessive, especially if it wastes sunshine. All that's really needed is 60 cm, enough space to comfortably walk, work or pull a kid's wagon through with tools or to collect the harvest. If plants do overflow into the aisle, draw your shears and teach them who is boss of the garden. Spacing is of course ultimately up to the gardener, aesthetics and sunshine.

To keep raised bed aisles free of unsightly weeds, strip out any turf and line the ground with horticultural fabric, sometimes called weed cloth. The fabric is inexpensive, comes in 1.2 m widths and needs only to be cut to size with scissors. Over the fabric, lay down a walkway of pre-cast pavers or old bricks, or a layer of crushed brick, pea gravel or coloured stones. The aisles will

Construct raised beds with more than one level to add aesthetic interest.

be weed-free and pretty, especially with pavers or brick. I would avoid putting down a layer of black plastic rather than weed cloth; it is slippery when wet, and anything placed upon it is sure to move around. I also eschew straw or pine mulch; loose organics are relatively cheap, but they stick to your footwear in a most annoying fashion.

The best time for constructing and filling raised bed gardens is during fall. By doing it then, gardeners will be ready to plant come spring. Just make sure to cover the soil with plastic sheeting so as to keep out wind-blown weed seeds over winter. With an early start in mind, it would benefit the square metre gardener to fix short lengths of PVC tubes to the sides of the frame to hold flexible wood or plastic arches so the beds may be cloched or covered with clear plastic sheeting in spring, shade fabric in midsummer and perhaps bird netting as the harvest season approaches (see Plant Protection, p. 103).

At the time of this writing, there is a company in Oregon that will deliver fully planted raised beds to customers and hook each one to a drip irrigation system. It's a very neat, hands-clean approach for people wanting fresh, pesticide-free produce but are constrained by time. It's a good idea, and it won't be long before it moves north. In the meantime, get building.

No special tools are necessary; just a drill and some screws.

3-square-metre Shallow Raised Bed

Materials

- (3) 8' long, 2" x 12" cedar, redwood or Douglas-fir boards
- (12) 3" long, galvanized wood screws
- tape measure
- pencil
- saw (or have the lumberyard cut one board in half)
- power drill and screwdriver

Assembly

- If you did not have the lumberyard do it for you, cut one board exactly in half.
- Measure 1" from the end of one long board and draw a line. Repeat at the other end of the board, and then do the same on both ends of the other long board.
- Drill three holes equidistantly along each of the four pencil lines.
- Butt your shorter boards between the ends of the long boards. When the tops are flush, screw away.

> **Note:** Attaching a 2" x 6" board across the tops of both ends will add strength to the beds and provide a handy seat, but is strictly optional. Attaching 1" x 2" pegs at the corners, cut sharp and a few inches longer than the boards are wide, will also add strength and foundation to raised beds when pounded into the ground, but is optional. Square metre gardeners wanting a slightly deeper bed may employ 3" x 16" boards of cedar, redwood or Douglas-fir constructed in the above manner, using longer screws and adding 4" x 4" corner braces for strength. Raised beds may also be adapted for ground that slopes by simply cutting wider boards to match the degree of slope.

Once the shallow frame or frames are constructed, they can be set in place. Orient your bed in either a north-south position so both sides receive sunshine, or a east-west position so all plants are facing south (tall ones in the back, short ones in the front). Do not place shallow raised beds over ground that tends to puddle after heavy rains; instead, construct the more substantial, higher walled deep beds for those areas.

Take the time to prepare the area under a shallow raised bed, then fill it with quality soil.

With the raised bed in place, the next step is to prepare the planting area. If your raised bed is being placed on existing lawn, the turf inside the frame needs to be removed. Simply use a garden edger to edge along the inner perimeter of the frame and cut the interior turf into strips, then use a spade to pry up the turf and remove it. Remove the soil inside the frame to a depth of 15–30 cm, level it out and shovel in pea gravel to a depth of 5 cm, spreading evenly. Pea gravel is for drainage and is easily acquired from lumberyards or from soil delivery companies. Then fill in your bed with a good quality planting soil.

Don't fill it right to the top edge; you'll need some room to plant. An optional addition to shallow raised beds is a screen at the bottom to keep out any burrowing critters, such as moles and voles. If you choose to use a screen, put it down before adding the pea gravel.

If the soil under your sod is not clay and is in good condition and has tested negative for heavy metals, turn it over with a garden fork to a depth of 20–30 cm and forego the layer of pea gravel. However, in most Canadian cities, soil will contain some traces of heavy metals because lead, mercury and cadmium were paint ingredients for centuries and have weathered into urban soils almost everywhere. Your property may have been the site of a smelter or metal depot during the World Wars, so unless you know for absolute certainty your soil is free of contaminates, remove it and replace it with fresh. It's a bit of a pain, but the soil will be working for you on a long-term basis so it might as well get off to a good start. Either way, you'll still need to fill in the bed above ground level with a good quality planting soil.

Square metre gardeners must become acquainted with soil structure, fertilizers, manures and composts. Garden soil is more than just dirt, and knowing

your growing medium will yield huge rewards come harvest time. For more on soil, see page 58.

3-square-metre Deep Raised Bed

Materials

- (12) 8' long, 4" x 6" cedar, redwood or Douglas-fir boards
- (28) 6" long, timber lock screws
- tape measure
- pencil
- saw (or have the lumberyard cut four boards in half)
- power drill and screwdriver

Healthy soil produces healthy plants; all the preparation labour will be worth it at harvest time.

Use sturdy boards when constructing deep raised beds.

Assembly

- If you did not have the lumberyard do it for you, cut four boards exactly in half.

- Find the centre on the narrow, 4" side of a short board and drill one screw hole through and into the end of a long board. After making sure the edges are flush, set your screw.

- Find the centre on the other end of that long board and drill one screw hole through and into the end of a different short board. Make sure those edges are flush, and set your screw.

- Continue alternating until the rectangle is complete.

- The next row is easier; continue alternating, but set your boards and drill and screw down through the top board into the bottom board.

Use two screws per corner, one in the long board and one in the short board.

- Keep going around, short end to long side, drilling and screwing from the top until the four layers are complete.

This is a substantial bed to hold substantial soil, and there is no cutting of turf required. Simply build, fill with soil and Bob's your uncle.

> **Tip:** Canadian winters take a toll on wood, and to get a few extra years out of yours, a coating of organic water-based wood preservative or linseed oil is recommended, with perhaps a stain added for the exteriors. Eschew all ideas of paint, as bits will surely flake and wind up in your salad.

Aesthetic appeal and good produce—raised beds have no downside.

The Nutshell

The aim of the square metre gardener is to have a sturdy, aesthetically pleasing frame or frames to contain high-quality garden soil to a depth of at least 30 cm. For growing vegetables, 30 cm is considered the standard depth. The frames may be shallow or deep, thick- or thin-walled, rustic or modern and can vary in height for aesthetic, physiological or topographical reasons, such as uneven or low-lying ground.

Soil lying under the 30 cm of fresh soil must be free draining; if that soil is clay, it will act as a barrier and water won't drain freely. Clay soil must be either removed or amended with organic matter and topped with pea gravel. The caveat to removing clay soil is that the depression may become a sump to migrating rainwater. Digging an exploratory 30 cm deep hole will be the determining factor on how to proceed. The exploratory hole will tell you the soil type and whether there is any danger of pooling water. If the hole fills with water after a few days, then construct a deep raised bed with wider, thicker boards.

Remember that raised bed gardens will become permanent fixtures on the property. Care taken during construction to make them attractive and long-lasting will pay off, especially when they are supporting the most attractive, best-tasting produce on the planet.

Containers

There is a container to fit any style, budget or spot of sunshine.

Gardeners who are extremely limited when it comes to space will likely be forced to grow all of their vegetables in containers. But it's not all bad news. Containers come in all shapes and sizes, in nearly unlimited materials, colours and styles. They are portable and can be moved to follow sunshine. Growing in containers means that almost any space that gets sunshine can be growing space.

Container gardening has always been popular with urbanites. Almost anything capable of holding soil has been suborned to grow flowering plants or trees: antique watering troughs, cement bird baths, sinks, bathtubs, etc. You name it, and it's been found, bought, dragged home and drilled for drainage. I have seen all manner of containers supporting all manner of plant life, and while a few contributed tremendous panache to cozy gardens, the majority lacked aesthetics, the most memorable being a footed bathtub filled with pink and purple petunias that I encountered whilst attending a garden party. The most aesthetically pleasing planters that I've seen have always been architectural salvage pieces, such as the gargoyle-fronted stone horse trough that served as summer home to a substantial Meyer lemon tree—now that was real panache. When selecting planters,

This hollowed-out rock makes a very pretty container.

go for the aesthetically pleasing, especially when planting vegetables or fruit trees. Architectural salvage pieces are the ticket, and if you're lucky enough to stumble across an iron or stone horse trough, grab it and start looking for a Meyer lemon tree. Almost all Canadian cities have an architectural salvage yard, so look there for your horse troughs and birdbaths, always keeping your space in mind. A large container will not fit into just any space.

For gardeners hard pressed for space, a single staked tomato plant will provide a lot of tomatoes for salad ingredients and burger toppings, while a single melon plant will yield multiple desserts. Almost all vegetable plants will do well in containers; a few, such as kale and Swiss chard, even have decorative

attributes. Beans and peas can be trellised or poled at the back of a large container while other vegetable plants occupy the front portion. Just make sure the climber does not shade out the other plants.

Free-standing containers are what most people think of when they think of container gardening, but there are other types of containers built for specific uses and spaces. Railing planters, window boxes, wall pots and hanging baskets all make use of vertical space. Faux raised beds are an excellent alternative to free-standing containers for people with enough room for several containers but not necessarily a full-size, 3-square-metre raised bed. Potato boxes are the best way to grow spuds; see below for easy instructions for building your own.

After constructing one or more raised beds, gardeners may want to try their hand at small deck planters for herbs, large deck planters for banana, fig or citrus trees and railing boxes for pepper plants, cherry tomatoes or flowers. Do an internet search for deck or patio planters to find designs; most are an easy build and incorporate various methods to keep soil from running away, such as screens or horticultural fabric over drainage holes.

Had your fill of woodworking? Then buy aesthetically pleasing containers at some of the more ambitious garden centres that stock all sizes and material combinations: pressed fibre in black iron stands, terracotta pots, stone pots, all sorts of synthetics, etc. Or go flea-marketing or antiquing; retro horse troughs will all add panache to the main event: the great deck-to-table dinner salad.

Vertical Gardening Containers

For balcony and deck railings, eschew those shallow "made in China" plastic rail hangers; they are for geraniums and petunias, not vegetables. Flowers are nice, but most of them aren't edible, and why waste sunshine on inedible plants? Besides, watching your favourite salad ingredients grow from pip

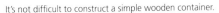
It's not difficult to construct a simple wooden container.

to table is far more exciting than a line of wind-dancing petals. Vegetable plants do more than look pretty; they entertain, educate and reward nurturing with tastes long missed or never experienced. In fact, almost everyone who tries a balcony-raised cherry tomato for the first time says, "Now that tastes like a real tomato!"

Railing boxes should be both aesthetically pleasing and substantial in size, as the more soil they contain the less often they will need watering.

The trick to window boxes is to either buy or build them aesthetically complementary to their location while also making sure they're functional. Long, narrow, plastic containers retailed as window boxes should be avoided. Instead, think like a European and install boxes that are large, robust and permanent. Although the European window boxes usually support voluminous mounds of flowers, there is no reason, except for a complete lack of sunshine, that these robust boxes cannot support a good number of different vegetable plants and herbs. In early spring, plant lettuce, radishes and Swiss chard, and when summer heat becomes oppressive, switch them up for various herbs, as most are heat tolerant and will excuse the odd drying out.

Wall pots are half-pots that are designed to hang on walls. If large enough and

Containers useful for vertical gardening include railing planters and hanging baskets or upside-down containers.

This wall pot is planted with flowers, but it could just as easily hold strawberries.

securely attached, they can be used to grow herbs and small vegetables, such as basil and cherry tomatoes, or small fruiting plants such as strawberries. The same types of edible plants can be grown in hanging baskets. Hanging baskets come in all sizes and materials; find one that suits your aesthetic tastes and make sure it is securely fastened to the ceiling or wall.

Faux Raised Beds

Gardeners need not reside in a house with a backyard to garden in raised beds. Simply place a bench along the balcony or patio wall and use wooden wine cases to frame soil—not deep wine cases, but the shallow ones used to pack fine wines on their sides. It's really container gardening Babylonian style. When set up properly they look amazingly like the real thing, especially when the vegetable plants are up and growing. Use one box for lettuce, another for radishes, etc. Make sure to drill plenty of drainage holes and cover the bottoms with plastic screen, then figure out where the water will go after it exits the holes. Onto the balcony floor is good because it will add humidity, but rivering over the edge will surely garner complaints from below, so be leery of wandering water.

Potato Boxes

Yes, you can grow potatoes in a 3-square-metre raised bed, but harvesting is a messy affair and why bother, when there is a better way to grow just as many: the potato box.

Materials

- (1) 2" x 2" cedar board, 12' long
- (6) 2" x 6" cedar boards, 8' long
- (96) 2½" long, wood screws
- tape measure
- pencil
- saw
- power drill and screwdriver

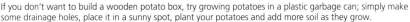

If you don't want to build a wooden potato box, try growing potatoes in a plastic garbage can; simply make some drainage holes, place it in a sunny spot, plant your potatoes and add more soil as they grow.

Assembly

- Cut (or ask the lumberyard to cut) the 2" x 2" board into four lengths of 3'.
- Cut (or ask the lumberyard to cut) the 2" x 6" boards into 24 lengths of 2'.
- Predrill all 2" x 6" sections, two equidistant screw holes 1" from the ends.
- Using the 2" x 2" sections as upright bracing for each corner, attach four 2" x 6" sections with wood screws to form the first layer of a box.
- Place the box in a sunny location over prepared soil and fill with raised bed soil.
- Plant 12 seed potatoes 4" deep, and water.
- After plants are up and growing 12" above bottom boards, attach four additional boards to form the second layer of the box and add more soil, making sure not to cover more than one-third of the stems.
- As the plants grow, keep adding boards and soil until the box is complete.

Harvesting

A few weeks after the box is completed, remove a bottom board, reach into the soil and pick out the finest spuds on the planet, then replace the board. When that layer is exhausted, remove a board from the second layer. Keep working up through each layer. It is a cornucopia of spuds and lots of fun.

Note: Potato plants in boxes will benefit greatly from drip irrigation. If not possible, water often without swamping. Potato plants also appreciate an occasional treat of organic liquid fertilizer with their water, such as fish emulsion or kelp. From setting out plants to the harvesting of full-sized potatoes takes approximately three months; spuds picked out early will be small to mid-sized.

This collapsible potato planter comes with a handy pocket for harvesting and easily folds away into storage in fall.

Preparing Containers for Planting

Drainage is all-important, so make sure there are enough holes to facilitate it. If there aren't, then drill some, or better yet, ask the seller to do that before you lay down the cash. Once you have the container home, clean it as best you can; scrub the inside with bleach and water. When the inside is thoroughly dry, cut a piece of plastic window screen to cover the drainage holes at the bottom. The screen will keep soil from draining out of the container along with the water. Then layer over a few inches of regular lump barbecue charcoal (not briquettes). Use a hammer to break up the larger chunks. The charcoal will aid in drainage and keep small soil particles from plugging up the screen covering the drainage holes.

Place a screen over the drainage holes to prevent the soil from running out with the water.

If containers are large, before you fill them, set them onto wheeled platforms or install castors on the bottoms. These are inexpensive and readily available at garden centres or packing supply stores. Fixing castors to large containers or setting planters on wheeled platforms will enable easy movement to make room for weekend barbecues or deck parties, and for the overwintering of tender herbs and fruit trees in the house or garage.

Fill your containers with potting soil or amended soil according to what is being planted: for woody plants already with roots, fill to half and add soil; for seeds or transplants, fill to the top, allowing a few centimetres for water. Soil for containers is necessarily lighter than raised bed soil to promote good air circulation and drainage, and gardeners may either purchase bagged soil specifically blended for container planting or amend raised bed soil with horticultural perlite or vermiculite. Do not use bagged topsoil without amending it with aged manure and compost because over time it will compact and become brick-like. For more on container soil, see page 63.

Container soil tends to dry out quickly, depending on volume. This should not be a problem once gardeners become tuned in to the needs of specific plants.

Vermiculite will aid in water retention, but even so, containers will need to be watered more often than raised beds. Large container plants, such as fruit trees and tomato plants, need plentiful water on warm, sunny days and less on overcast, cooler days. All vegetable plants are a thirsty lot, while most herbs actually prefer to be almost dried out between waterings.

Plants will grow as large as the roots allow, so gardeners wanting large vegetables in containers are advised not to overcrowd. If a really big cabbage is the end game, then plant a variety called 'Flathead Dutch' in a really big container and watch the fun. Oh, and if you're wanting to grow another cabbage in the same container next year, discard the old soil and sterilize the container with bleach.

Be sure to use potting mix meant for containers; it will resist compaction better than garden soil.

Tip: To combat the too-quick drying out of containers, build or buy them deep and include a layer of cut-up kitchen sponge in the soil.

A large vegetable such as rhubarb will do best on its own in a container.

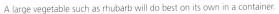

The Soil

Soil is all-important to plants. It provides both stability and nutrients. Healthy soil means healthy plants, so square metre gardeners are advised to pay close attention to what is going on at the root level of their plants.

Soil 101

Soil is made up of three basic particles: sand, silt and clay. Sand is rock material eroded by wind, water and glaciations into grains of various sizes: very fine, fine, medium, coarse and very coarse. Clay is rock chemically weathered by weak concentrations of carbonic or other acids leached from upper layers as in the formation of limestone caves. The individual particles are extremely small. Silt, sometimes called rock flour, is super fine sand usually formed through glaciations. These mineral specks—sand, clay and silt—in varying proportions make up about 45 percent of soil volume, while 50 percent is water and air and 5 percent is organic matter. That is the basic aggregate formula, the structure of soil, but as all gardeners know, most soils are far from perfect and need constant tweaking.

Soil across Canada varies greatly in its make-up and quality; most gardeners will have to tweak theirs to make their plants happy.

Earthworms are a sign of healthy soil.

Canadians are lucky; in large sections of the country the soil is home to all kinds of tiny creatures: bacteria, nematodes, rotifers, fungi, worms, etc. Lots and lots of tiny creatures, and all of them are hungry. Lumped together, they work like a stomach: macerating, digesting and expelling byproducts of organic matter. Left undisturbed, these microscopic creatures will produce the perfect soil aggregate, the right combination of minerals, water, air and organic matter necessary for healthy plant growth and stability. Without plant roots for stabilization, soil is at the mercy of weather and will break down and go with the flow, be it wind or rain.

Canada had soil stability in many areas, most notably on the prairie, with its endless sea of perennial grasses with deep root structures necessary for surviving winter, aerating soil and contributing organic matter to the aggregation.

All this changed in the late-18th and early-19th centuries, when settlers who knew nothing about farming or of crop rotation and resting the soil arrived to till the land and grow annual crops. Tilling and planting the same crops in the same fields year after year shrinks the aggregate size of the soil, and since historically a major drought can be expected every 20 years on the prairies, disasters occurred and many Canadian farmers were forced to abandon the land.

Today, the modern farmer avoids using the plow on fields in order to save the aggregate and conserve water. Nowadays, any field you see being worked over by a tractor is probably only having stubble chopped with a grain harrow after harvest. The farmer knows that to hang onto precious soil, he/she must protect it from wind and water erosion by not disturbing the organic mat left by the previous crop. So as not to disturb

Modern farmers know the value of soil and do everything they can to protect it.

the organic mat, farmers plant seed with non-intrusive air guns and reap huge benefits in saved labour and bushel per acre returns.

It's an interesting history, but square metre gardeners must concern themselves with soil that is not affected by natural processes; in other words, it will be up to the gardener to supply his/her plants with an ideal medium that contains all the necessary nutrients for optimum growth. Healthy plants mean an abundant harvest of fruits and vegetables packed with nutrients and tasting of almost-forgotten memories. Over time, all gardeners become obsessed with soil quality and receive much satisfaction formulating the ideal growth medium for their plants.

Raised Bed Soil

Screened triple mix is a mixture of top-soil, peat moss, sand and compost or aged manure, all mixed and run through a 12 mm or smaller screen. It is available almost everywhere and can be delivered in bulk or by the bag, in various quantities and qualities.

Buyer beware when ordering bedding soil; in every business there are unscrupulous dealers, especially during early spring when demand is highest. Take your time when ordering soil. Ask around, go online for information, and check out what is to be delivered before the delivery. Most soil suppliers located in or around Canadian cities are reputable and will go out of their way to assist your efforts to obtain the highest quality soil. Showing interest by way of

a personal appearance at their place of business may be profitable. Many companies reserve the finest black loam triple mix for their best or most interested customers or will make nutrient-added triple mixes specially formulated for raised bed vegetable gardening.

Many soil suppliers now deliver in convenient cubic metre "big bags" that can be deposited via a come-along forklift next to the raised bed or beds so that gardeners can simply cut open one side of the bag and fork out the contents. Eschew all ideas of having big bag soil deposited directly into the raised bed because this will undoubtedly result in damage to the frame.

Screened triple mix is quality soil, but making it perfect may require a little tweaking with a garden fork. Pick up

Even quality triple mix may require tweaking prior to planting.

a handful and give it a hard squeeze. It should be what is called friable and fall from your hand in the same manner as you picked it up. If it hangs together in a ball, more organic matter is required in the form of compost.

Raised bed soil is all about compost. Edible plants love it, and in return for goodly quantities they will deliver up the biggest, most luscious vegetables and fruits on the planet. If you have space, think about constructing a composter because an annual spring addition to raised beds is required. The larger the beds, the more compost will be needed every spring, and that spot near the garage will be perfect for your very own compost pile. See the Compost section (p. 67) for more information and details for constructing a composter that is both functional and aesthetically pleasing.

If a backyard composter is not feasible, use bagged compost along with a generous addition of blood and bone meal to keep the garden purely organic. Bone and blood meals are available at all garden centres, and all that is required is to

Give soil a squeeze to test its friability.

sprinkle some onto the bed or beds evenly before forking in the compost. If gardeners have concerns about bone and blood meals harbouring animal diseases, then a substitute of granulated kelp and horticultural lime is satisfactory.

Container Soil

If containers are additional to raised beds, gardeners can use the same screened triple mix soil, but they should mix in some vermiculite for water retention, as containers tend to dry quickly. If gardening a number of containers, buying bagged potting soil is the ticket. Make sure the product is formulated specifically for containers and contains vermiculite for water retention and perlite for drainage.

Perlite is a mined volcanic glass material that contains trapped water. When heated to high temperatures, the water vaporizes, exploding the heat-softened glass like popcorn. Perlite does not hold water, is highly porous and prevents soil compaction.

Vermiculite is a mined mineral similar to mica that, when heat-treated, reacts in much the same popcorn manner as perlite. But unlike perlite, vermiculite holds onto water like a sponge. A word to the wise: half of the world's supply of vermiculite came from a mine in Montana until it closed down due to asbestos content in the raw material. China is now a major world supplier of vermiculite, and because no testing is done on the contents of their product, gardeners are advised to wear a mask when handling vermiculite.

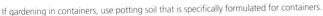
If gardening in containers, use potting soil that is specifically formulated for containers.

Soil Helpers

Along with screened triple mix, compost, aged manure and blood and bone meal, most plants need the assistance of microorganisms, such as mycorrhiza, and other micro- and macro-mineral elements, known as bio-stimulants.

Mycorrhiza

Mycorrhiza is a species of soil fungus plants need in order to prosper. When different species help each other they have what is called a symbiotic relationship, and the plant–mycorrhiza fungi help-fest has been going on for around 500 million years. Plants, especially the legumes, provide the fungus with carbohydrate sugars produced through photosynthesis and sent from their leaves to their roots, while the fungus provides plants the use of its mycelium for increased root surface area and better nutrient and water absorption.

It is an amazing partnership, and the addition of mycorrhiza inoculate to raised bed vegetable gardens will produce a marked increase in both size and quality of produce that will put big smiles on the faces of square metre gardeners. If you cannot find the product at local plant nurseries, it can be ordered online. Mycorrhiza should be sprinkled onto soil during installation and during spring turning, as well as onto seeds in a soak before planting (see Seed Treatment, p. 76).

All legumes, beans included, will benefit from the addition of mycorrhiza inoculate to the soil during planting.

Bio-stimulants

Bio-stimulants are naturally occurring minerals and organic matter not considered essential for plant development, but recognized as enhancers of plant growth and health. They are used extensively by commercial growers, and most bio-stimulants are available to home gardeners, including the following.

Triacontanol, also known as melissyl alcohol, is a naturally occurring plant hormone found in beeswax that is capable of boosting a plant's ability to photosynthesize sunlight. Add tiny amounts to fertilizer, and presto—you have a bigger, healthier plant.

Humates are the humic and fulvic acids found in peat and compost that is produced in commercial quantities from a low-grade, soft coal known as Leonardite. These naturally occurring chemicals are used as growth enhancers and can promote fantastic growth in plants, especially the fulvic acid. Humates work especially well with hydroponic systems and are widely used in commercial installations for both flower and vegetable production. Humates aid in photosynthesis and enable growth of extra healthy leaves, fruits and vegetables.

Not only are bees essential for pollination, but their wax also contains a hormone that aids in photosynthesis.

Peat moss contains humates, which aid in photosynthesis and root formation.

Humates also aid in root formation and contribute to the overall health of the plant. The humate source of choice for the square metre gardener will be the Leonardite, either in granular or liquid form—the former to be turned into the soil every spring along with compost, the latter to be added during watering. If using drip irrigation, a fertilizer injector should be employed.

Amino acids, derived from plant soy or sea kelp, can have a dramatic effect on plant growth when added to soil. Amino acids benefit local micro-flora, increase nutrient uptake by plant roots and contribute to the overall health of plants.

Salicylates, or common aspirin, when added to soil exhibit a hormone-like quality that aids in root formation and flowering. Aspirin also induces a resistance to various plant maladies and is a tried and true disease fighter for plants just as it is for humans.

Compost

My whole life has been spent waiting for an epiphany, a manifestation of God's presence, the kind of transcendent, magical experience that lets you see your place in the big picture. And that is what I had with my first compost heap.

—Bette Midler, actress and singer

The gardener's precious 3 square metres of raised bed soil is a living, breathing entity that requires sustenance in the form of organic matter, and the best organic amendments are aged manure and compost—the former as a replacement for used-up organics, the latter as daily plant rations. Both are intrinsic to raised bed vegetable gardening. Manure is turned into the soil during the fall months to allow soil organisms time to break it down into useable plant nutrients. Beware that too much manure will overload the soil with nitrogen, causing plants to grow leaves instead of vegetables. There can never be too much compost. Compost is pre-digested, enabling vegetable plants to take only what they need for optimum growth. It may be added anytime, either turned in or simply laid onto the surface as mulch.

This finished compost is ready to be added to the garden.

All plants benefit from the addition of compost.

The Benefits of Compost

- Earlier planting, as nutritionally rich soil is able to hold onto more heat than poorer quality soil. Inversely, this also allows for later harvest.

- Buffered soil, as the organic matter added by compost will ameliorate soils that are slightly acidic or alkaline, neutralizing pH to a level that is comfortable for most plants.

- Water retention, as compost-rich soil can hold many times the weight of water that poorer quality soil can hold.

If you don't want to build a composter, several models are available for purchase.

- Disease prevention, as nutritionally rich soil supplies plants with the micronutrients necessary to stave off viral, fungal and bacterial infections. Yes, plants do have an immune system, and compost is integral to its proper functioning.

Constructing a Wire Frame Composter

Square metre gardeners with adequate space may purchase composters in kit form at almost any garden centre. They come in many styles to fit the various needs of gardeners, with some even being aesthetically pleasing. Or gardeners may construct their own composter from a 3-metre length of concrete reinforcing mesh. Simply bend the mesh into a circle and clip it shut with all-weather zip ties, then place the frame in an out-of-the-way spot in the yard.

Begin filling the composter with compostable stuff (see below), layering brown and green materials. When it is full, simply pick up the frame and move it to another location to start the process over again. The finished pile will be there to use as needed.

Gardeners can speed up the action of their composter by frequent turnings with a garden fork, and for even faster action can add a little extra nitrogen in the form of cottonseed or soybean meal. Finished compost, the black earthy stuff, migrates down. When finished compost is wanted, get it from the bottom of the pile.

When not aesthetically pleasing, any composter can be made so by planting a few melons around the base. Melon plants love being around working compost and will send vines up, over and around, turning your composter into a leafy bower.

Gardeners with no room for a composter can purchase bagged compost at any garden centre.

Compostable Stuff

The Brown Stuff

- Dry plant materials
- Shredded newspaper
- Nut shells
- Woodchips or sawdust
- Hardwood ash

The Green Stuff

- Fresh plant materials
- Vegetable and fruit scraps
- Coffee grounds and tea bags
- Seaweed

The Not-for-Composting Stuff

- Garden weeds
- Diseased plant material
- Meats or fish
- Cooked vegetables
- Dog and cat poop
- Ashes from three-hour firelogs

Try to add a mix of brown (dry) and green (fresh) materials to your composter.

What, When and How Many Seeds

Ideally, the square metre gardener will have his/her soil prepared in fall and covered with plastic to prevent contamination by wind-blown weed seeds.

While the bed waits, gardeners will be figuring out what vegetable seeds to plant, when to plant them and how many of them to plant.

The Rules of Seed Buying

The first rule of seed buying is proper planning. The square metre gardener must know exactly what and how many plants they want and have room for and not be led down garden paths by online seed catalogues trumpeting new and interesting seed varieties. Make a list and stick to it; otherwise, you may end up with more seeds than can ever be planted, or seeds for plants that won't do well in your area or simply aren't practical.

Make a list and stick to it when buying seeds.

What produce the beds will provide is up to the gardener, who will know who likes what and how much. Democracy is the rule for planting choices, as there is little to be gained by planting vegetables no one is going to eat. Don't bite off more than can be chewed. For beginner vegetable gardeners, a good rule of thumb is to plant what is liked best, eaten most and easiest to grow, and allow those good people who man the booths at farmers' markets to supply any missing produce. Gardeners who find interesting produce at those markets can consider including that vegetable plant in next season's crop.

When planning, focus on plants and varieties that offer maximum yields from limited space. Cabbage is great, and it takes to raised bed culture like

fish to water, but one cabbage takes up space that is capable of producing a bushel of salad greens. Planting is intensive in 3-square-metre gardens; to get more bang for the buck despite a space constraint, some planning is required. Where to place containers and raised beds is rather up to you and your sunshine, but for some help with high-yield plant placement within a 3-square-metre bed, read the Spacing Seeds and Transplants section (p. 81) carefully.

Another rule is to make sure to choose indeterminate seed varieties and not dwarf or bush varieties. While many garden gurus advocate growing determinate bush plants to maximize plant placement and sun exposure and to minimize pruning and other maintenance, those choices require a trade-off

One cabbage takes up a lot of space; consider focusing on higher-yielding crops instead.

in quantity and taste. Square metre gardeners wanting the best-quality vegetables are advised to eschew the short and bushy for long and luscious, and all the plants ask for is a bit of support (see Raised Bed Vertical Gardening, p. 92).

Finally, before you buy, make sure seeds are fresh. Seed packs will be date stamped, and only the most recent should be considered. When buying seed packs well in advance of planting, make sure to store them in a dry environment. Most seeds will keep two to three years if properly stored in an airtight container with a handful of rice.

Heirloom Seeds

In search of my mother's garden, I found my own.

–Alice Walker, author

Canadians are well aware of what modern agricultural practices have done to commercial produce, and square metre gardeners will want to ignore vegetable seeds even remotely connected to the commercial raising of vegetable crops. Those are the over-hybridized, closed-pollinated seeds so often trumpeted in the pages of commercial seed catalogues. The vegetable plants that grow from them are inbred, and their seeds may not duplicate or breed true to the parent plants.

Open-pollinated plants (the heirloom varieties that your grandparents grew) are subject to pollination by winds or passing insects and may produce seeds that grow into plants that are slightly different from the parent plants. This is a good thing, as diversity often provides vegetable gardeners with exceptional produce.

An online search for open-pollinated heirloom seeds will provide a staggering

Look for heirloom seed varieties like these 'Nantes' carrots.

array of suppliers, which is beneficial to square metre gardeners because it allows the choosing of heirloom seeds from locally grown plants. Over time, plants become accustomed to a particular environment, with their offspring seeds becoming even more accustomed or acclimatized. A good example of acclimation is the very southern paw-paw tree. That tree has no business growing in southern Ontario, but grow it does, and has acclimatized so well that during the 19th century, a few orchards were established to provide Ontario residents ample supplies of its glorious fruit. Those orchards are now only a memory, but a few trees survive in backyards, their acclimatized seeds waiting for some ambitious farmer to replant the orchards.

Do purple or yellow tomatoes taste any different than red ones? Grow some and find out. Or simply try some procured at a local farmers' market, and if they elicit a "Now that tastes yummy," save those seeds for raised bed planting next spring.

Tomatoes are so much more than red; try growing a yellow variety.

Colour Up with Vegetables

Green denotes plant health, and most gardeners strive to raise vegetable plants of the deepest shade of green. This works for row gardens, but for gardeners with multiple square metre beds or expansive decks with multiple containers, the repetition of green can become blasé. Not to worry—most vegetable plant families have members with colourful leaves. Swiss chard is available in a variety of colours including red, purple, yellow, orange and white, and it can be interplanted to add splashes of colour throughout the garden or to create designs. Cabbage can be purple or red, late-season cauliflower can be yellow, pink or red, radishes may have red or purple leaves, radicchio is red and white, lettuce can be red, and tomatoes and peppers can spark sunshine in all colours of the rainbow: "Hey Martha, you planted so many vegetables with coloured leaves that the garden looks like a 1960s psychedelic poster."

Coloured vegetable plants will add pizzazz to raised beds, decks, balconies and rooftops and will allow the eight percent of Canadians who are colour blind to see their garden plants in colours other than drab shades of pink and yellow.

Swiss chard is one of the most colourful vegetables there are.

Planting Seeds

The rule of thumb is to place seeds into soil to a depth of three times the seed height, but because of exceptions to the rule, make sure to read the planting instructions on seed packets.

Square metre gardeners have three choices when planting seeds: plant indoors and transplant seedlings into raised beds or containers after the danger of frost has passed, plant seeds directly into raised beds or containers when soil temperature is apropos (check seed packets for recommended temperatures for planting seeds), or purchase ready-to-plant seedlings.

Whether you start seeds indoors or direct seed into your beds and containers outdoors often comes down to the length of your growing season. Many vegetable plants need a longer growing season than Canada provides, and in those cases, seeds will need to be started indoors or the plants purchased as seedlings. If you don't have the time or the space to start seeds indoors, purchase seedlings only from reputable growers owing to possible viral and bacterial contamination of soil.

Fast-maturing and hardy plants can often be direct seeded. When planting directly into raised beds or containers,

Heat-loving peppers will need to be started indoors or purchased as seedlings.

gardeners may hurry along the warming of soil by draping beds or containers with clear plastic. This method can also be employed to protect seedlings from frost as a temporary cloche, but don't forget to remove the plastic in the morning, or the sun will roast them to oblivion.

Radishes are a cool-weather crop that can be direct seeded outdoors (above).
Soaking seeds prior to planting will speed up germination (below).

Seed Proofing

Seed proofing is an unnecessary step when planting seeds purchased from reputable companies, but handy when using stored seeds (they will keep for two to three years in a dry environment). Seed proofing tells a gardener whether the seeds intended for spring planting will germinate or whether they have gone bad. Simply fold three or four seeds into blotting paper or paper towel, moisten with water and keep moist until the seeds germinate, usually a week to 10 days, but some seeds take much longer. If the sample seeds don't germinate, forget planting the rest.

For found seeds, or seeds that have been around for more than a few years, use more blotting paper and proof all the seeds destined for planting, discarding the mouldy and ungerminated.

Seed Treatment

This step is optional, but to speed up germination and kill latent pathogens, pop seeds into a pot of almost-boiling water, then turn off the heat and allow the seeds to soak for 18 hours. The initial heat will kill any pathogens, and the soaking softens the hard outer husk of seeds, enabling quicker germination. Adding a small amount of liquid organic fertilizer, such as fish emulsion, to the cooled soaking water will also help along seed germination.

For bean and pea seeds, a sprinkle of rhizobium inoculate will provide them some valuable friends down the road. Rhizobia are bacteria that carry on a symbiotic relationship with plants from the legume family, which includes peas and beans. Legumes supply the bacteria a home in the cells of their root nodules and various nutrients produced through photosynthesis; in return, the bacteria gather nitrogen from the air for the legumes to fix to root nodules. Rhizobium bacteria are probably already present in raised bed soils; however, to make sure of adequate populations when growing beans and peas, it is advisable to add inoculate to seeds before planting. Rhizobium inoculate can be purchased at most upscale garden centres or ordered online. Simply spoon a tiny amount of inoculate into the seed pack and give it a shake. Or, if soaking seeds prior to planting, add a small amount to the cooled soaking water.

> **Note:** There is a rhizobium inoculate for beans and a different one for peas. You need inoculates specific to each species.

Starting Seeds Indoors

Use plastic planting trays, either divided into cells (my favourite is the Speedling) or undivided, to start seeds. If different seeds are to share an undivided tray, do not forget to mark what is where because sprouted seedlings all look the same. For limited plantings, plastic deli containers or egg cartons are ideal, but don't forget the drainage holes. Seeds destined to become large plants, such as cabbage, broccoli and tomatoes, fare better when started in peat discs. The planting medium can be either raised bed soil, a soilless mix of equal parts perlite, peat and compost with a bit of sand, or straight vermiculite.

Bean seeds will benefit from a sprinkle of rhizobium inoculate.

First, sift the soil to make it easier for the little guys to get roots down. Use a horticultural sifter or a kitchen sifter and fill the planting tray to 1 cm from the top. Then dampen with a spray bottle and gently press flat. That done, sprinkle seeds onto the surface in a uniform manner and cover with 0.5 cm of sieved soil or vermiculite. Press down gently, dampen again with water from the spray bottle and cover the tray or container with plastic wrap or the clear plastic covers that can be purchased with the trays.

Now set the planted tray or container in a warm (21° C is ideal), dry spot and wait for seeds to germinate, 6–8 days for presoaked seeds and 10–12 days for dry, depending on the kind of seed. Do not place trays or containers on a sunny windowsill, or all will be lost. Once the seeds have germinated, remove the plastic covering and move the tray or container to that sunny windowsill or place it under grow lights, making sure to mist often with the spray bottle. Temperatures may be lower for sprouted seedlings, especially during evenings, as they will need some acclimatizing or hardening off before transplanting them outside.

Seed-starting supplies (top); plastic-covered seed tray (middle); seed tray under a grow light (bottom)

Plants destined to remain indoors for a while, such as tender, heat-loving tomatoes, peppers and eggplants, should be moved into 15 cm diameter pots for the duration, while the rest of the seedlings, such as hardy greens, can be moved into the garden once they have grown a second set of leaves. To remove seedlings from trays or containers, use a pencil to loosen the soil, take hold of the top leaves with thumb and forefinger, and gently pull. Use the pencil to wiggle a hole into the raised bed soil, place the seedling into the hole, cover with soil and tamp down gently with aforefinger. Do this a few times and even the novice gardener will become an expert planter. After all of the seedlings are into the soil, water with either a hose and misting attachment or a watering can with a rose spout, or turn on the drip irrigation. In other words, water gently and often for a few days until the seedlings are established.

Up-pot seedlings that will be indoors for a while to prevent them from becoming root-bound.

Lettuce is a cool-weather crop that can be direct seeded in early spring and again in fall.

Optimum Soil Temperatures for Direct Seeding

Insert a probe thermometer (inexpensive and available at most garden centres) into your soil. When determining soil temperature, ensure that the temperature is constant over a few days and not a fluke spike on an unusually warm day.

Cool Crop Seeds

The optimum soil temperature for seeding peas, lettuce, onions, radishes, spinach, Swiss chard, turnips, cauliflower and celery is 10° C. Lettuce, radish and pea seeds may be planted at lower temperatures, but you're taking a gamble as some may fail to germinate.

Beet, carrot, cabbage, parsley, kale and parsnip seeds are best planted when soil temperature reaches 13° C.

Summer Crop Seeds

Tomatoes, beans, eggplants, cucumbers, peppers, rutabagas, zucchini, squash and melons may be planted when soil reaches a temperature of 16° C.

Planting Schedule for Seeds and Transplants

Spring Planting Schedule

- 4–6 weeks before last anticipated spring frost: broccoli, cabbage, cauliflower, lettuce, onions, parsley, peas and spinach

- 4 weeks before last frost: beets, carrots, kale, radishes and Swiss chard

- On or about last frost: beans, summer squash and tomatoes

- 2 weeks after last frost: cucumbers, eggplant, melons, peppers and winter squash

Fall Planting Schedule

- 14–16 weeks before first anticipated fall frost: broccoli, cabbage, carrots and cauliflower
- 8–10 weeks before first frost: beets, lettuce, radishes and spinach

> **Tip:** For a continuous harvest of vegetables, sow seeds in staggered 10-day intervals.

Spacing Seeds and Transplants

Raised bed gardens, when filled with quality soil, are so efficient at supplying vegetable plants with all the necessities of life that their root systems stay small, compact and uncompetitive, allowing for intensive planting. Intensive planting means planting plants in closer proximity than what is called for on seed packets—about 25 percent closer. They should also be equidistant from each other, meaning the centre of one plant will be the same distance from all surrounding plants. Gardeners can do this by staggering rows. Intensive planting will create a solid canopy of foliage to shade out weeds and conserve water, a kind of living mulch. However, planting intensively requires due diligence on the part of gardeners to prevent insects and diseases from getting a start; gardeners must get right into the leaves and conduct regular inspections or risk losing the entire bed.

Beets are another cool-weather crop great for intensive planting.

Intensive Spacing Chart

The following chart gives the recommended spacing for intensively planted edible plants.

Plant	Centimetres	Plant	Centimetres
Asparagus	40–45	Kale	25–45
Beans, bush	10–15	Kohlrabi	15–30
Beans, lima	10–15	Leek	7–15
Beans, pole	15–30	Lettuce, head	25–30
Beets	5–10	Lettuce, leaf	10–15
Broccoli	30–45	Melon	45–60
Brussels sprouts	40–45	Onion	5–10
Cabbage	40–45	Peas	5–10
Cabbage, Chinese	25–30	Peppers	30–40
Carrots	5–7	Potatoes	25–30
Cauliflower	40–45	Radishes	5–7
Chard, Swiss	15–23	Rutabaga	10–15
Collards	30–40	Spinach	10–15
Corn	30–45	Squash, summer	45–60
Cucumber	30–45	Squash, winter	60–90
Eggplant	45–60	Tomatoes	45–60
Endive	40–45	Turnip	10–15

Intensive planting will provide high yields but requires some maintenance on the part of the gardener.

Saving Seeds

All gardeners have done it: saved seeds from a particularly good vegetable plant only to find the leopard has changed its spots after the plants from those seeds are up and producing. Vegetable plants go through a long process of hybridizing before their seeds will breed true and they are popped into packets, a process that entails keeping them on the straight and narrow sexually. There is no fooling around in the fields of commercial seed companies; pollination is controlled and accomplished by an army of rented bees that are in and out of there in a few days or less.

Home gardeners also depend on the ubiquitous honeybee for pollination, but unlike the bees used by commercial seed companies, our bees are vagabonds touring the neighbourhood and visiting every flower they can find. It's a good thing too, because without bees, gardeners would be forced to hand pollinate with a paintbrush. And hey, so what if the saved seeds produce fruit or vegetables like in the neighbour's garden; they could be bigger and better tasting, and that's another good thing. And so what if saved hybrid beefsteak tomato seeds grow up to become like their mother or father; those plants must have been spectacular to spawn the mighty beefsteak.

Seeds from backyard gardens or farmers' market produce need only be dried to preserve them. Drying is a natural process that most seeds require before they can germinate. When seeds have air dried properly, they should crack or break when bent; if they just bend, dry them longer. When dry, which usually takes a week to 10 days, pop them into a sealed jar along with some rice or

Try saving home-grown tomato seeds and see what comes up next summer.

To collect pea seeds for next year's planting, simply leave the pods on the vine to dry before picking them.

those little packets of silica gel. Then immediately write the seed name on the jar with a marker, because a failure to mark will undoubtedly cause problems down the road: "Hey Martha! Forget trying to remember what these are, we'll plant them anyway and call them forgetzees."

To save tomato seeds, scoop them from fully ripened fruit and place them into a jar of water for five days of fermenting. Just give the jar a swirl two or three times a day, and when the seeds sink to the bottom, the process is complete. Pour the liquid through a kitchen sieve, give the seeds a rinse, dry them on paper towels and spread them out on a tray or plate to finish air drying.

Pea and bean seed pods may be left on vines until dry and the seeds inside make a rattling noise—they may then be left in the pod or removed. Peppers may also be left on the vine until over-ripe and wrinkled; then remove the seeds and spread them out to dry.

A word of caution: carrots will cross-pollinate with their wild and weedy rel-ative Queen Anne's lace, also called wild carrot, and may produce seeds with the characteristics of both plants. To avoid surprises and culinary disappointment, gardeners are advised not to save carrot seeds if Queen Anne's lace is around—and it will be, since the plant is omni-present: "Hey Martha! Those saved carrot seeds you planted are looking a bit strange."

Optimizing Space

All gardening is landscape painting.

–William Kent, English garden designer

Ideas to create an illusion of space in tiny gardens are legion: build 3-square-metre raised beds to create interest and entertain the eyes; use bricks (perfect if they match your house) or small pavers for raised bed aisles and pathways; prune or remove overgrown shrubs or trees; and make a pathway to nowhere—just a quick turn disappearing into a tomato trellis.

Big or small, real or an illusion, the following planting techniques and ideas will help square metre gardeners make the most of their garden space.

Create the illusion of space by using paving stones to build a path to nowhere.

Intercropping

Intercropping helps keep weeds down and deters pest insects.

Intercropping is simply the socializing of various noncompeting vegetable plants. It is an agricultural technique long practiced in tropical countries, where all manner of vegetables share the same plot of land with coconut trees. Intercropping helps deter insect pests; because most insects are crop specific, mixing plant families gives them a less expansive target. It also helps keep weeds down by minimizing exposed soil.

The most common form of intercropping is to sow faster-maturing plants in the spaces between slower-growing plants. Once the early crops are finished, they are removed and the space becomes available for the slower-growing plants to fill in. If erecting a fence for beans, peas or other climbers, or employing cages for an entire bed of tomatoes (see Raised Bed Vertical Gardening, p. 92), gardeners may use the initial areas of empty space for planting fast-maturing, cool-crop vegetables such as lettuce, spinach, arugula and radishes. By the time the climbers need the space or have leafed out and blocked the sunshine at soil level, gardeners will have cropped out their salad vegetables, maybe a few times if started early enough.

Tomatoes and spring onions are a perfect match; the onions are ready to dig while the tomatoes are still climbing the support. Peas and beans are another good pair, with the peas being picked while the beans are just sending tendrils toward the sisal fence, poles or trellis. Lettuce and kale also get along famously; by the time kale leaves are large enough to shade out the lettuce, gardeners will have already cropped it twice.

Succession Planting

Hurry up and sleep, we need the pillows.

–Ancient Yiddish proverb

Succession planting is a technique useful for prolonging the harvest of fast-growing vegetables for a consistent supply. It is similar to intercropping, but a little different in that after harvesting your early, fast-growing plants you can either immediately sow them again or replace them with a different plant altogether. Pop out the harvested cool-crop vegetable, such as climbing peas that have run their course, and use the space for heat-loving cucumbers, zucchini, eggplants, small squash or melons.

Gardeners with cloched raised beds may do this a number of times with various vegetable plants, depending on the weather. Gardeners growing their own seedlings for transplant can keep a few growing and ready to pop into whatever space becomes available. As summer wanes and temperatures begin to fall, pull all the remaining summer-crop plants except tomatoes and cabbage from the raised beds and replace them with early varieties of cool-crop seedling transplants. By constructing a cloche for the raised bed or beds, gardeners will ensure a ready supply of salad greens right into winter (see Plant Protection, p. 103).

Plant heat-loving squash in the space left by cool-crop peas.

Staggered sowing, in this case of lettuce, ensures a steady supply and that no space is wasted.

planting seeds or seedlings at staggered times will provide gardeners a constant supply of ready-to-crop leaves for the salad bowl with no waiting for the grow-back. A neat method for staggering is to plant both seeds and seedlings; that way there will always be leaves for the salad bowl.

Simply staggering planting times also extends the harvest. Cut leafy salad greens and they will grow back, but

Note: Succession planting puts a strain on soil nutrients, so before replacing plants, fortify the soil with compost and organic fertilizer.

Companion Planting

The idea that vegetable plants have social likes and dislikes just like people do is a myth, but some garden plants do make for better companions than others. It has to do with nutrient requirements, but the relationships aren't always completely understood.

Carrots and tomatoes share some kind of give and take relationship, with tomatoes doing all the taking, but the why of it is a mystery and an anomaly. No one knows exactly what tomato plants draw from the carrots, but planting the two together will result in bigger, juicier and sweeter tomatoes, and carrots only half the size they should be, but still tasty.

And while it is true that members of the onion family exude sulphur and other noxious chemicals that can permeate soil and stunt the growth of legumes, that process takes years. If onions are intercropped with beans, they are always up and out before the beans get started. No harm done.

Although carrots may be stunted when grown with tomatoes, they will still be delicious.

Cops in the Garden

Companion planting is a good thing, but for a reason other than species likes, dislikes and competition, and that is helping gardeners control insects. Certain plants act like cops patrolling your garden, keeping it safe from pesky insect criminals. For example, in spite of being listed as a non-companion to nitrogen-fixing legumes by some garden writers, eggplant will actually benefit from a close proximity to beans because the legumes somehow repel Colorado potato beetles, which adore eggplant to the point that they have become a major problem for commercial growers. Other insect-controlling plants include the following.

Ladybugs are every gardener's friend; plant cilantro to attract them.

Marigolds exude insect-repelling chemicals.

- Cilantro will attract ladybugs, which are some of the best insects to have around. And everyone likes cilantro—well, maybe not everyone.

- Dill will repel aphids, spider mites and squash bugs.

- Geraniums will lure egg-laying cabbage moths away from the cabbage, broccoli and cauliflower.

- Lettuce planted alongside radishes will deter pesky ground flies from chewing on the radish foliage.

- Marigolds are both a visual delight and a mighty weapon against crop predation by many insect species, as they exude repelling chemicals. The flowers can even be used as a tasty ingredient for salads and as a cheap replacement for saffron.

- Nasturtiums planted near cucumber vines will deter attack by cucumber beetles and attract various predator insects to devour most garden bugs. A champion among predators is the ladybug, a cute little insect with a mighty appetite, especially for the gardener's curse, the sap-sucking aphid. Aphids will eschew all other plants for nasturtiums, and this preference provides gardeners a bug trap, as any infestation may be countered by removing the nasturtium plant, bugs and all, from the garden. Nasturtium flowers are also a favourite of honeybees, and planting some will ensure adequate pollination of all garden plants, while their colourful flowers will add colour and pizzazz to both garden and dinner table.

- Oregano repels flea beetles, and a container placed near vine crops is beneficial.

- Sweet alyssum flowers attract large numbers of predator insects that feed on garden pests, and butterflies love the tiny white flowers. How sweet is that? The plant can be invasive, but it is easily controlled by pulling.

- Sage planted in a container and placed near cabbage, beans or carrots will repel loopers and cabbage flies.

- Tarragon is repellent to white flies.

While many garden writers advocate the use of companion plants as part of the raised bed complement, I recommend keeping the herbage locked up in containers to prevent it overrunning the neighbourhood. Companion plants that flower—the nasturtiums, sweet alyssum, geraniums and marigolds—add pizzazz to raised beds, but don't go overboard; plant them along edges and in corners. If space is a constraint and you can't plant them all, go with nasturtiums.

Nasturtiums will act as a trap for aphids.

Growing in Partial Shade

Most vegetables require full sun, but if full sun is at a premium in your garden, as long as you have partial shade you are in luck. Leafy vegetables, such as lettuce, kale, arugula, Swiss chard and spinach, thrive in partial shade and will produce a longer lasting crop than they would if grown in full sun, as too much heat causes premature bolting. Bolting is a plant's sudden switch from growing leaves to producing flowers; it's a reaction to stress (usually from overheated soil), and it mostly ruins a plant for table use. Bolting may be guarded against by quick action with scissors or garden snips, an action that gave rise to the saying "nipped in the bud." Snipping off flower stems before they get going will usually teach plants who is the boss of the garden and have them back to growing leaves.

Root vegetables, such as carrots and beets, may be grown in partial shade. They will yield smaller produce at harvest time, but the baby vegetables taste as good as their full sun mates. Onions may be grown in shade if the produce desired is scallions.

Vegetable Plants for Partial Shade

A minimum of four hours of daily sunshine will see these plants to maturity,

Spinach is just one of many leafy greens that thrive in partial shade.

but both plants and their produce will be smaller than those grown in full sun.

- Arugula
- Beets
- Carrots
- Chinese cabbage
- Kale
- Lettuce
- Mint
- Parsley
- Peas
- Radishes
- Rutabagas
- Scallions
- Sorrel
- Spinach
- Swiss chard

Raised Bed Vertical Gardening

When the going gets tough, the tough grow up. Vertical gardening is a great way to save space in your raised beds.

An obelisk provides an attractive support for climbing vegetable plants.

Many vegetable producing plants require support in the form of an upright or arched trellis, fencing, tripod, netting or cage. Climbing is an evolutionary adaptation by certain plants, such as tomatoes, beans, eggplants, zucchini and cucumbers, to rise above the habitat of mould, disease and crawling insects. What they rise upon is up to the gardener.

> **Note:** All climbing plants welcome a little help in getting their tendrils to weave in, out or around whatever climbing support the gardener supplies.

Tuteur and Tent Line

Probably the easiest and most aesthetically pleasing support for gardeners not interested in becoming the neighbourhood tomato sauce depot is the French

A line of tuteurs provides support in a raised bed.

tuteur, or tripod, an especially helpful adjunct for growing climbing crops in a manageable style. The tuteur is simply a teepee made from three or four bamboo poles angled firmly into the soil toward each other and tied together at the top. Several tuteurs could be placed every few feet in a raised bed.

Designed primarily for growing indeterminate tomato plants, which continually grow and produce for an entire season, the tuteur is easily adapted for cucumbers, beans and other climbers by connecting the teepee tops with narrow poles. On this frame gardeners simply lean a series of thin bamboo poles (available at all garden centres) to form a tent six or seven poles to a side (about 15 cm apart) and secured to the cross member with twine (they don't call them pole beans for nothing). Gardeners will want to plant six tomato plants under each teepee, with cukes, beans, peas, zucchini, etc. next to the thin bamboo poles in an orderly fashion. In other words, don't mix them up; plant them in sections, one side in cukes and zucchini, the other side in two or three bean and pea varieties. Confining beans and peas to one side will mean gardeners will only have to add small amounts of kelp or fish emulsion fertilizers to one side and the ends of the bed because the beans and peas are legumes and fix their own nitrogen.

The tuteur and tent line is a powerhouse that will generate a constant supply of large, luscious vegetables right into fall and keep fresh air circulating among the leaves so as not to encourage moulds. Gardeners can forego the tent line and stick with a single tuteur, and simply plant around the poles (as many as six) and train plant tendrils to climb those poles.

Sisal Fence

Another support method for gardeners wanting to devote an entire 3-square-metre bed to growing climbers is to erect a pair of woven fences from sisal or plastic twine. Simply pound four sharpened poles into the ground, two each at opposite ends of the bed equidistant from each other, with perhaps another in the centre for added support. Higher poles mean more beans, but keep the tops within reach. Connect the poles with a length of twine strung from one top to

If you don't want to weave your own sisal fence, plastic mesh works just as well.

the other, and tie securely. Repeat, working down at 10 cm intervals, leaving a 20 cm space at the bottom. Then start the up-weave, tying the twine to each cross twine as you go. It sounds daunting, but it's actually quick and very easy, as weaving the second fence will demonstrate.

If you're not into weaving, then single or double strands of twine will do just fine. If you're really not into weaving, use poly netting, chicken wire, dollar store badminton nets or concrete reinforcing mesh. But, practice makes perfect, and weaving another sisal fence for cucumbers, zucchini, beans or peas should be a snap—pun intended.

Tomato Cage

The most common method for helping tomato plants get off the ground in raised beds is the tomato cage. They come in many sizes, but square metre gardeners will want cages as close to 60 cm in diameter as possible to fit side by side into the west end of the raised bed to prevent shading of other crops, or to fill the entire bed. Large, collapsible tomato cages that allow for one cage to be fitted on top of another are available, and these are perfect, especially for a small number of indeterminate tomato plants, as they will grow as high as the gardener allows while producing fantastic tomatoes. Gardeners wanting to save some money can make their own tomato cages from concrete reinforcing mesh—simply bend the mesh into a circle and fasten it with all-weather zip ties.

> **Tip:** Before winterizing (with plastic sheeting) a raised bed, turn a shovelful of hardwood fireplace ash into the soil in those areas meant for tomatoes, peas and beans. Just make sure the ashes are from hardwoods and not pine or three-hour firelogs.

Tomatoes grow well in containers, as long as they have adequate support.

Planting on the Edge

Planting on the edge is about making use of unconventional spaces to optimize growing area. I have a friend who resides in a condominium so ritzy that nothing is allowed on the balconies. Most condo associations are more broad-minded and allow for some vegetation but may draw the line at railing planters or stipulate that they must be hung inside rather than outside of railings. Gardeners residing in condominiums are advised to check what is allowable before installing any plant material. Condominium rooftops have become popular gardening sites, with some associations providing amenities such as raised beds and convenient water sources. Apartment dwellers have no association rules to deal with, but may be constrained by property managers as to what is allowed on balconies, window ledges and fire escapes, so check first and avoid disappointment later.

Condo dwellers must make use of whatever space and sunshine is available to grow their plants.

Balcony Gardens

There are five rules to balcony gardening: use the correct plants for the space; use proper sized planting vessels; do not overcrowd the planting vessels; adhere to aesthetics; and make sure there is a convenient water supply.

Balcony gardeners must take available space and sunshine into account when selecting plant material, with four being the magic number. If the sun stays in one spot for at least four hours, the cultivation of many vegetable plants is possible. They may not be large and will take longer to mature, but large plants look out of place on most balconies, and longer isn't all bad as leaves from salad plants can be picked anytime once they are half grown.

Strawberries are perfect balcony plants.

Any sunny balcony can become a lush, productive garden.

Tomatoes need more. Balcony gardeners will want tomato plants, and any wall with seven hours of sunshine is perfect for indeterminates; simply erect something for them to climb, and in no time at all there will tomatoes for picking. However, because sunny walls are balcony rarities, gardeners may have to forego the wall for staked plants in a corner or a determinate bush plant sitting centre stage.

Mapping available sunshine is the thing to do (see p. 34 for how). Your sunshine map will tell you what plants should go where and how many. Gardeners with east-facing balconies may add an extra hour to the map for reflective light, while those facing west have the pick of sun-loving, heat-ameliorating vegetable plants. Those gardeners with north-facing balconies are out of luck as far as vegetables and are advised to install a few coniferous shrubs. Balconies in between, facing northeast or northwest, can add an hour to the map simply by painting the balcony white. Installing a mirror at one end of the balcony will not only increase sunshine hours but will also add an illusion of spaciousness.

Don't forget about the railing and walls. An empty balcony or fire escape railing basking in sunshine is almost a crime, especially when there are vegetable plants almost custom made for railing planters, such as cherry and grape tomatoes. Small tomatoes are easy to grow and easy to prune for height, are non-cracking, will produce fruits more quickly than their larger relatives, and will keep on producing right into fall. If safety permits, hang railing planters on the outside as it frees up inside space. These plants also do well in hanging baskets or wall pots; just make sure they

Herbs are low-maintenance plants great for beginner gardeners.

are large enough (30 cm diameter is good), drain well and are strongly bolted to the ceiling or wall.

Remember the two magic words—"water" and "fertilizer"—for to forget either one means to shrivel and die. To keep from becoming a water slave to the balcony, consider installing vegetables in self-watering containers (see p. 112), as they permit leaving home for short vacations. As for fertilizer, bagged soil formulated especially for containers never has enough essential nutrients, so make sure to lay in a good supply of liquid organic fertilizer, such as fish emulsion. When transplanting seedlings either purchased from garden centres or started on a windowsill, sprinkle granulated organic fertilizer, such as kelp or seaweed, into the planting hole and then sprinkle some on top of the soil after planting.

If new to gardening, walk before running and plant only a few experimental containers. Next season you will know the meaning of the word "seasoned" and can turn the balcony into a jungle of vegetable plants. Salad vegetables are a good bet, as are tomatoes, cucumbers and peppers.

Heat-loving peppers are ideal container plants.

Containers on a deck can supply produce all season long.

Deck Gardens

A large deck with adequate sunshine can supply a family with fresh produce for an entire growing season. If space permits, downsized raised beds can be installed for salad vegetables, and for the space-constrained there are faux raised beds, the wooden wine boxes (see p. 53). Decks often have wide railings that permit hanging boxes outside, inside and on top, while the inside space can be aesthetically dotted with large and small containers for growing everything from cabbage to sealing wax. I'm not kidding about the wax; a potted dwarf bayberry bush will not only provide wax for sealing a few letters (if that's your thing), but it will also keep away bugs and add flavour to barbecued steaks and roasts. A potted dwarf citrus tree will provide a topic of conversation while guests munch on bayberry-flavoured steak and anticipate sampling the fruit hanging from the banana tree. Almost any plant material can be grown on a deck, be it exotic or workaday produce, and mixing them up adds aesthetic interest.

Wall pots placed here and there against the house wall and planted with cherry or grape tomatoes will also contribute to the aesthetics, as their trailing tendrils soften the line between house and nature.

Sunny wall space can be growing space simply by placing containers and trellis along that wall.

Wall and Fence Gardens

Tomatoes, cucumbers, melons, egg-plants, runner beans and zucchini can be grown on walls or fences that receive full sun for six to eight hours daily. Ideally the space should be south facing, where light reflection and retained heat will combine to produce some amazing vegetables. Wall and fence gardens can be as simple as a trellis placed in a container of soil onto which will climb a single tomato plant, or, with planning and a bit of work, an entire garden of climbing plants growing from a long, narrow raised bed.

Getting plants to adhere to walls and fences is not difficult and can be as easy as tacking up chicken wire or polyethylene netting above a container or a long, narrow raised bed. It may be a bit of an eyesore to start, but once the plants get a grip and begin climbing, the wall will be transformed into a jungle of vegetable-bearing stems and leaves. Jungles can be problematic; they are hot and humid and they spawn diseases. An air space will fix that; simply tack some batting onto the wall every few feet and attach the chicken wire or netting to the batting.

Rooftop Gardens

I have known many people lucky enough to have access to flat rooftops for gardening purposes, and they all made the same first-season mistakes: too many plants, an inadequate water supply and a failure to anticipate rooftop weather conditions. Summer in the city can be a sweltering affair, but on flat roofs sweltering is early morning, turning unbearable by noon. Wind is another problem; a windy day at street level is a hurricane on rooftops, and without some kind of windbreak, off go the tomato plants and everything else not nailed down.

To be master of an empty rooftop is to be King Nebuchadnezzar of ancient Babylon sans engineers to solve the water problem. Finding a water faucet on a rooftop supplies meaning to the word "pipedream"—it ain't gonna be there. Hopeful rooftop gardeners will need both a plumber and the building owner's permission to tap into the water main, because any other method, such as running a hose from an apartment sink, is just another pipedream.

Dealing with rooftop weather conditions can be challenging, but getting it right can be very rewarding.

Prospective rooftop gardeners must compile a checklist: sun protection, sturdy stanchions to support that protection, windbreaks, walkways, a drip irrigation system, etc. The list is long and gets longer depending on the size of the installation, so starting small and working up is wise; it's going to take time to get it right. Rooftops are becoming ever more popular gardening spots, with many participants recording their experiences via online blogs; check them out for tips and inspiration. Do not be put off by difficulties; if the rooftop is yours for the working, use it, but remember to start small. Or, if money is no constraint, hire an expert.

Window Gardens

It's a lucky tenant who has an outside window ledge to garden, as most modern buildings have either window stops or they open out rather than up and down. But even the unlucky have the inside ledge for growing all manner of culinary herbs.

Or the entire window can be used for growing through a system called "window farming," wherein salad greens and herbs are cultivated in a hanging curtain of plastic bottles that are supplied with water and nutrients by an aquarium pump. Gardeners may acquire information online at www.windowfarms.com.

A windowsill is a great spot to grow herbs or leafy greens, along with flowers.

Taking Care of Your Plants

To get the most out of 3 square metres, gardeners will have to perform some basic maintenance tasks. These include protecting plants, both from weather and predation, watering, fertilizing and regularly patrolling for pests and diseases. None of the tasks is diffiult, and a little maintenance goes a long way to producing a healthy, bountiful crop of vegetables.

Plant Protection

Most of Canada has a relatively short growing season, but there are simple ways for gardeners to extend it by protecting plants from frost. Plants may also need protection from predation or too much heat. The best of these methods is cloches and hoop tunnels, but floating covers and cold frames are also useful.

This hoop frame can be used to support plastic for protection from frost as well as the netting currently being used for protection from pests.

Cloches and Hoop Tunnels

Cloche is what the old-time French gardeners called temporary, heat-trapping plant covers, usually bell jars or cut wine bottles. In modern times, with the invention of clear polyethylene plastic sheeting, the word has come to mean a temporary greenhouse, also called a hoop tunnel, employed by commercial vegetable farmers to protect crops from early and late frosts.

Canadian square metre gardeners seeking to maximize crop production are advised to follow the farmers' lead and erect a cloche or hoop tunnel over their raised beds. Besides frost protection, a cloche will serve to warm soil and provide gardeners an early start for seed germination. Not difficult to erect, the cloche in its simplest form is merely a frame of flexible plastic hoops over the raised bed to support a sheet of 6-mm polyethylene plastic for as long as desired. Then again, the square metre gardener may want something that, while still simple to construct, is a bit more robust for duties other than frost protection, such as supporting shade cloth to protect plants from sunburn during midsummer heat waves, or netting to keep pesky birds and small critters from nibbling the crops.

To construct a very simple cloche for a 3-square-metre raised bed, use three 2.5 cm diameter, 1.8–2.1 m long, flexible PVC pipes attached to both sides of the bed with pipe strapping (all available at most any hardware store), or

A plastic bottle can be used as a cloche for a single plant.

Use flexible piping to create a hoop tunnel over your raised bed.

simply stick the ends of the pipes into the soil next to the frame sides, bending them to form arches; either method is serviceable. Drape the pipes with 6-mm clear plastic and secure it with nails and rubber washers. A high wind may have you buying more plastic sheeting. Longer pipes make higher arches; commercial growers employ very long pipes to construct temporay greenhouses.

To construct a more robust cloche, I suggest an online search. There are dozens of great models, one of my favourites being Oregon State University's Extension Service site that features a money-is-no-object tutorial on constructing a combination raised bed and cloche. Square metre gardeners considering a greenhouse or conservatory may want to adopt that design, as it's almost a greenhouse and is a very progressive first step toward gardening under glass.

Gardeners residing in high-traffic urban areas should consider installing a cloche to protect raised beds from air pollution and tire dust, as both are sources of toxic heavy metals absorbed by many vegetable plants.

Floating Covers

Floating covers are simply lightweight plastic sheets, shade cloth or bird or insect netting that can be thrown over raised bed crops, no hoops required, to counter particular threats. If a late spring cold snap is imminent, cover the bed with plastic, weight down the edges and remove when the warmth returns. For midsummer heat waves, throw over the shade cloth. Insect and bird netting can be employed to counter invasion. Floating covers are inexpensive and may be purchased by the roll or cut to order at garden centres or online supply companies. When a particular threat is over, simply roll up the covers for reuse if threats return.

Bird netting is PVC mesh (like the bags fresh oranges come in), and it does a good job keeping out birds in a humane, no tangle manner. It can easily be cut to size with scissors and is available at most garden centres. Gardeners wanting longevity in bird or insect netting will want 25-mm, PVC-coated wire mesh netting, preferably manufactured in Canada or the U.S., as it will outlast cheap Chinese imports by years. However, cheap Chinese netting works fine for the short term, and both come in rolls of various widths and will protect crops from insects and birds, but not small four legged critters, hail or midsummer sunburn. If you have cloche hoops installed, simply remove the clear PVC sheeting and replace with netting. The permanent installation of netting would most certainly solve most insect problems, but at the expense of produce, because insects visiting vegetable plants in flower provide pollination.

Hoops aren't necessary for floating covers, but they do give plants room to breathe.

Cold frames have largely fallen out of use in favour of cloches.

Cold Frames

Cold frames are simply raised or sunken soil frames with a glass or clear plastic top. In days long gone, gardeners would employ old windowed doors hinged to a frame and sunk into the ground. Cold frames are still employed for early starting of plants, hardening off, and to protect them from early and late frosts, but square metre gardeners are advised to use the more sensible cloche for those purposes.

However, if you want a very early start, you can turn a cold frame into a hotbed. Simply dig a hole, dump in a few pails of raw horse manure, cover with soil and place a cold frame overtop. After a few days, the decomposing manure will begin to give off heat, and salad greens can be planted.

Irrigation

Gardeners new to the game must pay special attention to water requirements until a line of communication is opened between plants and gardener. No kidding, plants are very good communicators and will tell you when things are wrong in the water and grub department; all gardeners must do is listen.

In the meantime, get into the finger-poking habit and feel for moisture. Gardeners with window boxes have it easy; they simply water every morning as they greet the new day. Later, as the crops mature, they will water again just before lunch, as they pick luscious vegetables for the noonday salad.

Getting water to your vegetable plants can be as simple as plugging a spray nozzle onto a garden hose or as technically advanced as a drip irrigation system with a manifold faucet connection and timer.

Hose and Nozzle

Some gardeners love this method and find it therapeutic to be so hands-on, but most others find it tedious and will usually end up watering everything in sight to relieve the boredom. Readers with gardening experience will have seen this before: a wife asks her husband to water the plants on the deck while

she goes shopping, and upon returning finds the entire deck submerged.

Gardeners are a sociable lot and love to visit and show, and while large gardens are simply shown with pride, the small jewel-like creations must first be given a good washing down with the hose. The numbers of dripping-wet gardens I have visited are legion, and there's no denying that the après-rainstorm treatment is effective, as everything is all shiny and fresh, but I always feel for the plants. Plants love a good dousing; so do moulds and other plant diseases that are bounced from soil to leaves by ricocheting water droplets. Do not hose

For a small number of containers, a rain barrel and watering can are a good option for watering.

A hose and nozzle is a very simple, inexpensive way to water plants.

down vegetable plants unless it's to rid them of an infestation of insects. Oh I know, plenty of garden gurus advocate spraying leaves for foliar feeding, but a wise gardener feeds the soil and not the plants.

Soaker Hose and Trickle Tape

A soaker hose is basically an extra-flexible, small-diameter garden hose stopped at one end, with tiny emitter holes along its length that drip water. Soaker hose is also available in a flat

trickle tape that is useful if water is hard, as the emitter holes will not plug up with minerals. Gardeners can purchase these hoses in various lengths at garden centres. Although it may be tempting to employ a used-up common garden hose as a soaker hose, doing so is not a good idea because the holes will become larger under pressure.

To avoid forgetful floods, do not even consider employing a soaker hose without installing a timer on the faucet. Timers are an inexpensive necessity and are available at most garden centres.

Wind soaker hose through a raised bed, and install a timer to avoid overwatering.

Drip Irrigation

Drip irrigation is the absolute best method for watering raised beds. Inexpensive drip irrigation kits are available at garden centres or may be ordered from online companies that offer prospective buyers helpful how-to video tutorials. Gardeners need only install a plastic manifold onto an outside faucet and attach a mainline plastic pipe that can be fitted with elbows for any bends and turns on the way to the square

Tap into an underground irrigation system if one exists.

metre bed or beds. The mainline pipe is secured along the way to the raised bed by wooden stakes with zip ties, and to one side of the raised bed frame with plastic clamps. To this mainline are attached tiny hoses fitted with drip emitters and spaced at whatever intervals the gardener desires—for square metre intensive gardeners, usually 15 cm. I know, it sounds like work for a plumber, but the installation is really a snap, a lot of snaps, but worth every one. Plants love not being water stressed and will offer up luscious rewards to thoughtful gardeners. Again, make sure a timer comes with the kit, for to be without is courting disaster.

Gardeners with installed landscape irrigation in the form of underground piping and risers may purchase kits that simply attach to whatever riser is closest to the square metre bed or beds. Once again, make sure the riser kit includes a timer.

Square metre gardeners installing a multiple raised bed drip irrigation system (sounds daunting, but is really a snap) may want to install a fertilizer injector. Large injectors are a necessity for commercial vegetable growers, but smaller versions are now being marketed for home gardeners. There is even a 1-pint injector that fits onto a garden hose. Injectors are also handy for adding bio-stimulants to soil (see Soil Helpers, p. 64).

While it is true that a spring preparation of raised bed soil needs no further fertilizing, tests prove that small amounts of organic fertilizers, such as fish emulsion or kelp, administered every few days will provide gardeners with larger, more tasty vegetables—and for this, a small fertilizer injector is perfect. Remember, use small amounts only; too much will have plants growing more leaves than vegetables or fruit. In other words, too little is better than too much. If using liquid kelp or fish emulsion, think capful and not a quick pour from the bottle.

Container Irrigation

If installing a drip irrigation kit for your raised beds, take note that adjunct kits for containers are available that take advantage of the already-installed main plastic water pipe. Thin plastic tubes with only one emitter at the end are simply snapped into the main line and run to the containers. For gardeners employing only containers, there are kits that simply attach to an outside faucet. Here again, a timer is advised to prevent forgetful flooding.

> **Note:** Testing the drip irrigation system is important because too much water is as bad as too little. Use the finger test; stick a finger into the soil, and if it comes out wet and muddy, cut back on the water until the finger comes out damp but clean.

Efficient drip irrigation kits for containers are available.

Mulch is great for water conservation, but it is labour-intensive to install.

Self-watering containers have a built-in water reservoir that allows plants to draw up water as needed through various wicking mechanisms. They can be as simple as two 5-gallon plastic buckets, one nested in the other (go online for instructions), or they can be purchased at garden centres in all manner of styles, materials and sizes. Large self-watering containers are perfect for those gardeners wanting an oasis of green with minimum effort, but they can be a problem if fill-and-forget is taken too seriously—plants will still need a bit of attention now and again.

Mulch

Covering any exposed soil with organic material, such as small wood chips, shavings, straw, dried seaweed, etc., will cut down on water evaporation and help to fortify the soil. That it works is undeniable, but there is downside: plants, especially vegetable plants, do not appreciate being touched by wet organic matter; it softens stems and stalks and allows access by pathogens. So, unless the gardener is willing to take the time to clear a circle around every stalk and stem, it is better to forget mulching, especially in intensively planted raised bed gardens, where plant leaves will act as living mulch and shade out all but the most determined weeds.

Inorganic mulch is aesthetically undesirable for raised bed culture, but it works fine when used in containers. A layer of coloured or polished stones can bolster pot pizzazz considerably.

Fertilizers

Most vegetable plants are heavy feeders, so to get the best produce, gardeners are advised to use some form of fertilizer throughout the growing season.

Inorganic Fertilizers

Inorganic fertilizers are the manufactured ones sold with three numbers on the bag. The first number refers to the amount of nitrogen (N) in the product. Nitrogen is a chemical common in the atmosphere. It can be produced by mixing air with methane gas and subjecting both to heat, pressure and a catalyst to produce anhydrous ammonia, which, when mixed with nitric acid, produces nitrate fertilizers. More than 100 million tons of nitrate fertilizer is manufactured annually around the globe, using almost five percent of natural gas production. Nitrates come in various purities, but for agricultural use, the content is 20 percent or below—the first number on the fertilizer bag is usually 20. Nitrogen is essential for the production of amino acids, and soils lacking nitrogen will produce unhealthy, stunted plants.

The second number on the bag refers to the amount of phosphorus (P). When mined phosphate rock is ground to a fine powder and treated with sulphuric acid, water-soluble superphosphate is produced. Mining accumulated deposits of bat and bird droppings—called guano—is another method of obtaining water-soluble phosphate. Plants, especially seedlings, require phosphorus for cell division and growth of both tips and roots. Vegetable plants lacking phosphorus will be stunted and have weak roots.

Most vegetable plants are heavy feeders that appreciate fertilizer throughout the season.

The third number refers to the amount of potassium (K) in the product. Potash, the common name of the mineral potassium carbonate, is a mined or manufactured salt that contains water-soluble potassium, an element with many chemical variations, such as potassium hydroxide (lye) for soap making, potassium carbonate for glass, soap, leavening bread and nitrate of potash (saltpeter) for making gunpowder. The potash employed as a fertilizer is potassium chloride, or muriate of potassium: a mineral mined from ancient seabeds and clay deposits. Potassium is a necessary element for both people and plants, and Canada supplies the world with around one-third of its agricultural potash from mines in Saskatchewan. Plants need potassium to maintain moisture balance, resist disease, grow strong roots and produce large, succulent vegetables.

Too Much of a Good Thing…

Gardeners experienced with turf or flowers but new to growing vegetables may be tempted to share a box of quickie grow with the veggies: "Hey Martha! We're outta fish emulsion, but I have a whole bag of grass fertilizer."

Hopefully, Martha will put the kybosh on that idea. Grass fertilizer will contain high levels of nitrogen, which will cause

Do not use lawn fertilizer on your vegetables; it contains too much nitrogen.

Inorganic fertilizer may produce big tomatoes, but at the expense of taste.

vegetable plants to forget their reason for being and expend all that newly acquired energy growing leaves.

My Dad's Amazing Tomatoes

For my parents, to cottage or not was decided by a flip of the coin in favour of a swimming pool, a big one, with a diving board and a great latticework privacy fence that ran its entire length. The fence needed something, and while ivy was suggested, my dad opted for tomatoes—lots and lots of his favourite, the beefsteak tomato.

A few weeks later, the fence was magically half-covered in vines to rival the proverbial Jack's beanstalk, and they required no attention at all, no watering or fertilizing. They got water via cannonball; big pools attract kids who do cannonballs off diving boards, splashing lots of water.

A month later, the vines had covered the entire fence, both sides, and had begun to flower—lots and lots of flowers that soon begat lots and lots of tomatoes. Big had been expected, as they were all beefsteaks, but those tomatoes soon grew past the expected into the surreal, with some as big as my dad's swelled head whenever he showed off his magical crop to friends. "What do you feed them?" was always asked, but never answered; there was no answer to give.

It was a mystery, only answered the day of the first picking. Dad barbecued steaks and boiled fresh corn to accompany the perfectly formed, fire truck red, mother of all tomatoes. Family gathered around to fill their plates: steak, an ear of corn and a slice of Dad's pride and joy tomato. Forks went to the tomato, up to mouths went the forks, and in not two chews out came the tomato followed by a loud chorus of "Yee-uuuk!"

My dad's amazing tomatoes tasted of pool chlorine. Mystery solved. His amazing tomato plants had lapped up pool water like thirsty dogs and had taken up the chlorine (swimming pool water is disinfected with calcium hypochlorite, a form of chlorine and the stuff used to make household bleach) as chloride ions.

The moral of story: to avoid off tastes in vegetables, eschew inorganic fertilizers, as chloride is an active ingredient in most of them.

Organic Fertilizers

These fertilizers are soil nutrient compounds that are naturally occurring, such as aged manures, worm castings, guano, peat and seaweed. At various times during Canada's history, maritime

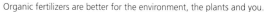

Organic fertilizers are better for the environment, the plants and you.

Organic amendments (left to right): moisture-holding granules, earthworm castings, glacial dust, mycorrhizae, bat guano, compost, bone meal and coir fibre.

commodities such as oysters, herring and lobster saw use as fertilizer. The last of that extravagance occurred during World War II, when all nitrate fertilizer production was switched to the manufacture of explosives. Some nutrient compounds require tweaking by natural enzymes, bacteria or a factory process, such as composts, blood and bone meal, humic acid, amino acids and liquid fish emulsions, along with seaweed, kelp and algae extracts.

Types of Organic Fertilizer

Plant Based

- Alfalfa and soybean meal both have an NPK (nitrogen, phosphorous and potassium) content of 3-1-1, with the alfalfa meal containing small amounts of triacontanol, a plant growth regulator.

- Kelp meal (1-0-8) is high in potassium, micronutrients and growth hormones.

- Liquid seaweed (4-2-3) meets all nutritional requirements and is high in micronutrients.

Animal Based

- Blood meal (12-2-1) is high in nitrogen and is especially good for leafy vegetables.

- Bone meal (2-12-2) is high in the phosphorus needed for strong roots, stems and fruit development.

- Fish emulsion (8-12-2) meets all nutritional requirements and is high in micronutrients.

- Aged manure (2-1-2) meets all nutritional requirements and is essential for soil conditioning.

A word to the wise: Milorganite, a popular lawn and garden fertilizer, is actually the incinerated sewage sludge produced by residents of Milwaukee, Wisconsin. Incinerated to 1000° F to kill pathogens, the product is relatively cheap and popular with golf courses, homeowners wanting to green-up lawns, and many vegetable gardeners. However, a recent shipment to Canada was refused entry because of salmonella contamination, while back in Milwaukee, concerns are rising over PCB contaminates in that city's effluent. Square metre gardeners are advised against using Milorganite on raised bed or container vegetable plants.

Compost and Other Household Wastes

Of the more than 50 micro- and macronutrients that vegetables require for optimum growth, a well-prepared and well-managed compost pile will supply them all. Urban gardeners who have no space for a composter can purchase compost in bulk or bagged from soil suppliers or garden centres, but the free compost given away by many cities is actually composted leaves and is more apropos for mulching.

Vermicompost, more commonly called "worm castings," is a good source of slow-release nutrients. It is too expensive for raised bed soil amendment, but it is useful as a tonic for vegetable plants

Preparing a vermicomposting bin is simple.

in containers. The City of Toronto, and probably some others, is actively promoting vermicomosting as a way for apartment dwellers, invalids and the time-constrained to compost wastes indoors. At this writing there are detailed raising instructions posted online, and I have little doubt that free worms can't be far behind: "Hey Martha! There's a guy at the door giving away worms. You want some?"

While adding some nutrient value, properly prepared compost is most essential for conditioning raised bed soil by adding organic matter. Either purchased or produced in a home composter, the stuff is essential to square metre gardening (see Compost, p. 67).

Hardwood ash contains no nitrogen and low levels of phosphorus and potassium, but it is a good source of calcium and trace nutrients needed for optimum plant health. Just make sure the ash is from hardwood and does not contain toxic remnants of three-hour fire logs.

Coffee grounds contain lots of nitrogen, and some high-volume coffee shops give them away to anyone who asks. However, coffee grounds do contain significant amounts of residual tannin, which acts as a growth inhibitor to many vegetable plants. Since looking gift horses in the mouth is never a wise move, gardeners/coffee drinkers are advised to use coffee grounds on plant material other than raised bed vegetable plants.

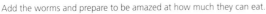
Add the worms and prepare to be amazed at how much they can eat.

Pests and Diseases: Knowing and Controlling Them

In the garden, some bugs are good and some bugs are bad; knowing the difference and taking action only against the insect pests is crucial to a healthy crop. A quick daily inspection will tell you who has taken up residence in your square metre beds, and whether any diseases are taking hold. Catching any problems early is half the battle.

Know Your Insect Friends

Assassin Bugs

These are good-looking guys, beetles in iridescent black tuxedos with yellow pinstripe edging. Gardeners should take care not to hurt any assassin bugs in their garden; on the other hand, gardeners should find out why any assassin bugs are there and what they're having for dinner.

Dragonflies

These insects are basically flying appetites, and if spotted hanging around your garden, that is a good indicator they have found dinner and you had better check what that might be, as it could be a threat if left unchecked.

Green Lacewings

These guys are about 2 cm long and a light green colour with golden eyes. Attracted by aphid honeydew, they lay eggs on hairy leaf stalks that hatch out larvae commonly called aphid lions for their ferocity in attacking aphids.

Green lacewing

Ground beetle

They're ugly little beasts, but if aphids threaten, they come to the rescue like cavalry.

Ground Beetles

Hundreds of species of these fast-moving garden predators call Canada home, with the most common being an import, the European ground beetle. These guys, both adults and larvae, hunt at night, and they will attack and consume any insect encountered, but they also attack beneficial earthworms, which is the only fly in an otherwise perfect ointment. These guys come in all sizes and colours, but are mostly black or iridescent green and 6 mm long.

Ladybugs

These cute little guys move about like hungry gypsies; when they find dinner, they will gorge and then move on, but not before depositing an egg cluster that will hatch out larvae that feed on aphids, mealybugs and various pest beetles. The larvae are spiny and brightly coloured, usually black with yellow spots, and though they look dangerous, they are harmless to people and a good friend to gardeners.

Adult ladybug

Ladybug larva

Praying Mantis

This guy is feared by all insects and will attack and consume any in reach, either big or small. Gardeners who find a praying mantis in their raised bed can sleep at night knowing there is a cop guarding the vegetables. If the cop has no wings, it's a junior mantis or nymph and it will hang around policing, but when it goes through a final molt and wings appear, it will fly off to search out better chomping grounds.

Spiders

Around 1400 species of spider call Canada home, and a few may find their way into your crop of vegetables, whether that crop is in a raised bed or a container. Probably they are transient visitors, just passing through looking for a meal, but if you should spot a web, most likely in a raised bed, you can thank your lucky stars. A web means that the web maker has found threats to the crop and has come to the rescue.

Spined Soldier Bugs

These guys belong to a family of insects commonly called stinkbugs and are the most common predator insects in North America. They go through six molts from nymph to adult and begin to feed after the second molt on just about any insect in sight, including the Colorado potato beetle and cabbage worms. Oh, and they're called stinkbugs because they squirt a noxious substance that smells like skunk, so better leave them be to go about their business.

Spider

Syrphid Flies

Also known as hover flies or flower flies, these little guys feeds on flower pollen and nectar but will deposit eggs when they find food—usually aphids or other soft-bodied insects—for their larvae. Syrphid larvae look like small caterpillars, but they are legless, tapered and have translucent skin usually with a yellow stripe down the back. Syrphid fly larvae are ferocious and will clean out aphids like a vacuum cleaner.

Wasps

Parasitic wasp species far outnumber people on the planet, but most gardeners are oblivious to their beneficial presence. That is because predator wasps patrol the undersides of leaves searching for, depending on species, either dinner or a fat insect in which to lay eggs for their carnivorous larvae. These tiny wasps are extremely beneficial to gardeners but can be wiped out by even the most non-toxic of pesticides.

Wasp

Japanese beetles (above); aphids (below)

Know Your Insect Pests

The following is a list of the most common edible plants grown in Canada and the pests that may be threatening your harvest of those plants.

- Artichokes: aphids
- Asparagus: asparagus beetles
- Basil: very few pests; a good companion plant
- Beans: cutworms, leafhoppers, Japanese beetles, June beetles, aphids, spider mites
- Beets: leaf miners, aphids, blister beetles, leafhoppers
- Broccoli: aphids, cabbage worms, cabbage loopers, cabbage root maggots, flea beetles, cutworms
- Brussels sprouts: cabbage loopers, cabbage root maggots, cabbage worms, flea beetles, slugs

- Cabbage: cabbage loopers, cabbage root maggots, cabbage worms, flea beetles, slugs
- Carrots: aphids, rust flies, parsley worms, tarnished plant bugs, nematodes, slugs
- Cauliflower: cabbage worms, cabbage loopers, aphids
- Celeriac: slugs
- Celery: parsley worms, thrips, tarnished plant bugs
- Chives: very few pests
- Corn: cutworms, flea beetles, Japanese beetles, earworms, borers, wireworms
- Cucumbers: cucumber beetles, squash bugs
- Dill: parsley worms
- Eggplant: flea beetles, Colorado potato beetles, Asiatic beetles
- Endive: very few predators
- Fennel: aphids, slugs

Colorado potato beetle

- Garlic: very few pests
- Horseradish: very few pests
- Kale: cabbage loopers, flea beetles, aphids, slugs
- Kohlrabi: cabbage worms, cabbage loopers
- Leeks: thrips, onion maggots
- Lettuce: aphids

Spider mite web

Slug (above left); snail (above right)

- Melons: cucumber beetles, squash bugs, spider mites
- Onions: thrips
- Parsley: parsley worms
- Parsnips: aphids, rust flies, parsley worms, tarnished plant bugs, nematodes, slugs
- Peas: leafhoppers, tarnished plant bugs

Leaf miner damage

- Peppers: aphids, cutworms, hornworms, leafhoppers
- Potatoes: flea beetles, leafhoppers, Colorado potato beetles, wireworms
- Radishes: flea beetles, cabbage root maggots
- Rhubarb: very few pests
- Rutabagas: very few pests
- Salsify: very few pests
- Spinach: aphids, leaf miners, flea beetles, caterpillars
- Squash: squash bugs, squash borers, cucumber beetles, aphids, whiteflies
- Swiss chard: leaf miners, leafhoppers, flea beetles, grasshoppers, slugs
- Tomatoes: cutworms, flea beetles, blister beetles, nematodes, spider mites, thrips, hornworms
- Turnips: aphids, cabbage root maggots, turnip mosaic virus

Organic Pesticides

Square metre gardeners will have little trouble with insect pests because plantings are intensive and small in area, making chance encounters with flying insects a rarity. But when local creepy crawlies go for the gold, gardeners have a small arsenal of controls and organic bug killers.

Because many pest insects specific to one species of plant overwinter in soil, it is a good idea to rotate vegetable plantings into different beds, or at the very least, a different spot in the same bed. Due diligence is the first line of defence for a square metre gardener. A daily inspection of the underside of leaves will supply gardeners ample warning that an infestation is underway. Find the bugs early and they can be hand picked, blown away by a hard spray from a garden hose or caught in sticky pheromone traps. Sticky traps work well to trap insects such as whiteflies, leafhoppers, aphids, thrips and miner flies. You can buy ready to hang traps, or the resin to smear onto duct tape. Traps checked daily allow gardeners a heads-up to insect threats.

If early controls fail, gardeners have heavier weapons. Natural sprays and dusts such as horticultural cornmeal can take care of cutworms, and by adding some salt to the cornmeal, cabbage worms are stopped dead in their tracks. For soft-bodied crawlers, including slugs and snails, a dusting of diatomaceous earth around the base of susceptible plants will have those insects sliced up like baloney. A dusting of boric acid, commonly called borax, will kill hardbodied crawlers such as earwigs, beetles, ants, etc., and help eradicate various moulds. Use natural pesticides sparingly and only when needed.

Sticky pheromone trap

Home-brewed Pesticides

When spraying any of these formulations, it is advisable to wear a protective mask.

Baking Soda

Just 45 mL baking soda dissolved in 7.5 L warm water, along with 30 mL each of dish detergent, canola oil and vinegar, will work to eradicate many insect species. This solution works best in early spring when insects are emerging.

Citrus Peel Extract

Stuff as many orange and/or lemon peels as you can into a large jar of water and soak for 24 hours. Mix the resulting liquid with a few drops of dish detergent to produce an effective decoction for eradicating mites, mealybugs and ants. Simply strain the liquid into a sprayer and soak tops and bottoms of leaves, preferably in early morning or dusk to prevent too-fast evaporation.

Citrus peels make an excellent spray for controlling pests.

Garlic spray will keep pests away.

Garlic and Hot Stuff

Garlic works wonders; simply drop six finely chopped garlic cloves into 1 L water, along with one chopped onion and 5 mL each of cayenne pepper and dish detergent (not green or organic dish soap). Allow mixture to steep for 24 hours. Strain and spray, making sure to cover all leaves, top and bottom. This spray works well on all insects, but for even more effectiveness, add 5 mL neem oil to the mixture.

Rhubarb Leaf Extract

The leaves of rhubarb plants are toxic to humans and insects alike, and growing some rhubarb will provide square metre gardeners a bounteous supply of delicious, non-toxic stalks along with their deadly leaves to extract the bug-killing components. Pop some leaves into a pot of boiling water, remove from heat and let soak 24 hours. Then run the liquid through a fine sieve, add a few drops of regular dish detergent and you have a most effective natural insecticide for mites and aphids.

Use caution; rhubarb leaf extract contains a large amount of oxalic acid that is toxic when ingested. Make it, use it all, and wear a mask while applying. If you must keep it around, mark the

Rhubarb is a very useful garden plant; the stalks are edible, and the leaves can be used to make an effective pesticide.

container with a poison symbol and lock it away. There is no chance of accidental poisoning of children, pets or adults by consumption of rhubarb leaves from the garden because they are extremely bitter; if they make it into anyone's mouth, they won't stay there long enough to do any harm.

Insecticidal Soap

This formulation will clear away many insect pests. To make it, simply mix 75 mL dish detergent into 4 L water and spray. Use regular non-organic, potash-based dish detergent because the organic dish detergent does nothing. Spray very early in the morning or at night to keep the soap from drying too

quickly, and don't forget to spray under the leaves. Gardeners may increase the potency and broaden the killing spectrum of insecticidal soap by adding 15 mL neem oil to the formula.

Dormant Oil

Dormant oil is similar to horticultural oil, but with added phenol compounds and tars. It is used basically to combat scale on woody plants. Not for use in raised bed vegetable gardens, it is only mentioned for its similarity to horticultural oil.

Horticultural Oil

Gardeners can buy a horticultural oil spray ready-made or make it themselves. Horticultural oil works by suffocating insect pests. The spray is made simply by mixing 15 mL canola oil and 5 mL dishwashing detergent (not organic and no special additives) with 4 L water. Shake well and spray, making sure to cover all areas of plants. It works especially well on aphids, thrips and whiteflies.

Neem Oil

Neem oil is expressed from the seeds and fruit of the neem tree, an evergreen native to India, and is a very effective broad-spectrum insecticide, miticide, bactericide and fungicide that works by breaking down the hormonal system of creatures. To make a spray, simply add 30 mL neem oil to 4 L water. Spray any infestations every day for two weeks, then reduce to once a week. Spray in early morning, making sure to cover all foliage tops and bottoms. Neem oil spray is especially effective in controlling fungus infections in leafy climbing plants, such as cucumbers.

Natural Biocontrols

Chitosan

Chitosan is manufactured from the chitin found in the shells of processed crab, shrimp and lobster. Not quite fertilizer and not quite pesticide, chitosan is a broad-spectrum bacteria and fungicide that improves plant growth and root structure when used as a seed treatment and in a watering program. It helps plants resist and fight off pests and diseases. Although it is not yet readily available in Canada, this should soon change. The Province of Quebec has begun to actively promote the manufacture of chitosan from the waste product of its shrimp fishery.

Predator Nematodes

These microscopic terrors invade the bodies of soil-dwelling insects that consume plants at the roots. Some nematodes are pests, but the good ones are great for destroying all manner of beetles, borers, grubs, worms and flies, and the wee beasties are readily available at garden centres or from online supply companies. Simply keep them refrigerated until needed, then mix with water

Predator nematodes can take care of the beetles that cause damage.

and apply during watering. For drip irrigation systems with fertilizer injectors, mix with water and load into the injector.

Diseases and Remedies

Most plant diseases are caused by moulds. Mould spores arrive at gardens on the wind and in many forms: powder, rust, black, yellow and brown spots, end rot, root rot and other rots. Chemical remedies to combat moulds are legion, but they are not for the square metre gardener because they tend to accumulate in soil and migrate into plants. One of the best organic remedies for moulds is the baking soda spray (see p. 128), but use it only on overcast days, early mornings or at night to prevent a too-quick drying of the solution.

Plants not in raised beds—shrubs, flowers, etc.—will benefit from a dousing of Bordeaux mixture, a simple combination of fine-ground lime and copper sulfate. Bordeaux is available as a ready mix, or you can purchase the ingredients at a garden supply store and make your own by following easy directions available online. Bordeaux mixture is organic, but it should not be used on edible plants because it contains copper.

> **Note:** After removing diseased tissue or leaves, always disinfect garden shears with alcohol, hydrogen peroxide or bleach to prevent transmission to other plants.

Black Spot

Black spot, also known as leaf spot or leaf blight (*Diplocarpon* spp.), is a perennial fungal curse of all gardeners, but it is especially vexing to rose cultivators because it tends to hang

Black spot

around from season to season no matter what remedial action is taken. Removal of infected plants is recommended, but only as a last resort. Copper-based fungicides, along with the removal of infected leaves, will go a long way to control black spot. Neem oil, a more natural method, will also help in control, but it is not as effective as some brand-name chemicals. Avoid wetting leaves, keep beds clean, and apply a good layer of mulch to keep infected soil from splashing onto leaves.

Botrytis Blight

Botrytis blight, also known as grey mould (*Botrytis cinerea*), is a fungus that will attack a wide range of garden plants: peonies, tulips, geraniums, grapes, etc. Look for discoloured leaves, wilted stalks and withered fruit. Good air circulation and clean beds will discourage botrytis blight, but once infected, remove stricken leaves and spray with a copper sulphate solution.

Early Blight

Early blight (*Alternaria solani*) is a fungal infection specific to tomato and potato plants usually started in cool, wet springs. The fungus begins on bottom leaves and works up, causing leaf yellowing and dropping, and undersized fruit and tubers. For control, prune bottom leaves, avoid wetting the plants, keep beds clear of debris, and rotate plantings.

Late Blight

Late blight is one of many diseases caused by a group of aggressive, parasitic semi-fungi called oomycetes that have the ability to move toward or away from chemical signals. One member of this group, genus *Phytophthora*, was responsible for the Irish potato famine and the demise of the American chestnut tree. Nowadays a fungus from this family causes damping off in seedlings and downy mildew, and mainly attacks potatoes, tomatoes and other members of that family of plants. Planting blight-resistant seed potatoes and tomatoes helps in controlling this scourge.

Damping Off

This disease is the ultimate depressive happening for gardeners who plant vegetable seeds directly into gardens. Sprouts are looking healthy and fine, then suddenly they thin at the base, wilt and die. Numerous fungi will cause damping off, and to prevent it happening, spray beds before planting with a strong solution of chamomile tea, or a solution of water and baking soda.

Fusarium Wilt

The fungus species *Fusarium graminearum*, sometimes called Panama disease, is the fungus responsible for the demise of the Big Mike banana during the 1950s and early 1960s. Banana growers switched to the Fusarium mould resistant, but inferior tasting,

Late blight is a threat to potatoes.

Cavendish banana now purchased in supermarkets. Mould resistant, yes, but it can still harbour mould spores, so make sure to wash your hands thoroughly after handling bananas before venturing into the garden. Fusarium mould has become a huge problem to western grain growers and has made its way into greenhouse crops, especially peppers.

Called Fusarium wilt in gardens, this mould blocks vascular tissues in plants and is noticeable as a fluffy white or pink growth on lower stems. If you find this disease, dig out the infected plants along with a good quantity of surrounding soil, bag and seal the whole and dispose of it in regular garbage.

Powdery mildew

Powdery Mildew

Powdery mildew is a fungus that can affect all manner of plants, but it is host specific, meaning the strain infecting one species of plant will not normally affect other species. Eradication is possible through removal of infected leaves, thinning or pruning stems, or applying an organic fungicide to the infected area.

For an effective organic spray for powdery mildew, add 500 mL strong chamomile tea to 4 L water along with 10 mL baking soda and 60 mL cooking oil. Do not fertilize garden plants until after the

fungus is eradicated, and avoid wetting the leaves when watering. If circumstances require the use of a non-organic chemical fungicide on raised bed vegetable plants, stop spraying two weeks before harvest.

Rust

Rust (*Puccinia* spp.) is a group of over 5000 fungi that do great damage to commercial field crops and garden plants. On the commercial front, wheat rust can become epidemic and wipe out entire crops, causing shortages and high prices of flour. However, and lucky for gardeners, each rust strain is species specific and targets only individual plant species, allowing other plants to survive.

All plants are susceptible to different rust infections, and the best protection is a sharp eye and the instant removal of infected leaves, which will be an orangey rust colour and have a velvet texture. Rake up all plant debris, sterilize any tools that come in contact with the fungus, and spray infected plants with insecticidal soap.

Rust

The Vegetables

For all things produced in a garden, whether of salads or fruits, a poor man will eat better that has one of his own, than a rich man who has none.

–J.C. Loudon, botanist and author

Bean and Pea Family

Leguminosae; legumes

Rhizobium is the name of the bacterium soil and seed inoculate that is recommended for growing legumes. Beans are either pole or bush varieties, the climbers and non-climbers, with the former being the recommended for raised beds because they enable intercropping. One teepee tent row of one or a mixed variety should suffice for a family of three people. Another row for peas would do the same.

Legumes are some of the most popular, prolific and easy vegetables to grow.

Broad Beans

Vicia faba

- Full sun, but will tolerate some shade

These are the fava beans, also known as Windsor, faba or field beans, and are among the oldest cultivated crops on the planet. They are easy to grow and cold tolerant, meaning seeds can be in the ground weeks earlier than other bean varieties, with a minimum soil temperature of 10° C. Seeds (beans) germinate in 10–14 days but can be soaked in water for a few days until sprouted and then planted. Not all seeds will germinate, and by soaking them first, gardeners will be assured that all plants that make it into the soil will be started. Fava beans require 15 cm of space and some support to keep them from toppling over.

> **Caution:** never consume uncooked raw beans, as many contain the toxic chemical lectin, which can make consumers extremely ill.

French Climbing Beans

Phaseolus vulgaris

- Strictly full sun

Also known as green, snap or pole beans, French beans will need a high sisal fence or tripod and canes because they are vigorous climbers. They will attain an impressive size and will cast a large shadow that is beneficial to intercropped plants such as lettuce and beets.

These beans are also easy to grow, but the sprouts are not cold tolerant and do best when started indoors or cloched. Sow seeds or transplant sprouts 15 cm apart, either around a single tripod, at the base of each bamboo pole in a tripod and cane setup, or along the bottom of a sisal fence. If sowing seeds, plant several, thin to the most robust and don't forget to help the young plants twine. Beans like plenty of water, especially during hot spells, and are self-fertilizing if rhizobium bacterium is present. Beans will be ready for picking in two months, and the more you pick, the more you get.

French climbing beans do well in large containers as long as there is plenty of organic matter in the soil and a pole to climb upon. Do not allow container beans to dry out, and they may need some additional liquid organic fertilizer.

Runner Beans

Phaseolus coccineus

■ Strictly full sun

These beans are more cold tolerant than French beans and can be seeded directly and earlier. Other than that, everything is the same. Get them planted early, and start picking in July right through to late fall. The more you pick the more you get, so pick lots and pick often.

Young runner beans will not be stringy and may be boiled in salted water for 6–7 minutes for a delicious side dish. Older beans will need stringing, but square metre gardeners need not concern themselves with older beans; surplus can be left to dry on the vines and harvested when the beans are hard in the shell—they will make a rattling noise when you shake the pod.

Peas

Pisum sativum

- Full sun, but late varieties will tolerate some shade

A hardier plant than beans, peas can withstand light early and late frosts and are perfect for intercropping with plants that prefer a little shade, such as lettuce, beets and radishes. However, when stressed by overheated soil during summer heat waves, the pea plant will often bolt, leaving gardeners disappointed. Square metre gardeners are advised to plant early, midsummer and late varieties.

Peas require a fence or trellis for climbing; plant seeds on both sides, 1 cm deep and 5 cm apart. Seeds will germinate in 1–2 weeks (soaked seeds germinate quicker) at a soil temperature as low as 5° C, so get them in early and at 10-day intervals to ensure a steady crop. If drip irrigation is not being used, make sure to mist newly emerged pea plants daily. During summer heat waves, apply extra water to cool the soil even when implementing a drip irrigation system.

Pea plants are available in many varieties of two types: standard English shelling peas and Chinese snow peas, the latter composed of popular subvarieties such as sugar or sugar snaps. English, or standard, peas are available in many cultivars with varied maturing times: earlies around 60 days, midsummers at 75 days, and late seasons at 90 days. Chinese snow peas and sugar snap peas will mature around 50 days, with the sugar snap being the most prolific pod producer of any pea plant variety so long as gardeners pick them.

> **Tip:** Birds are among the worst pea pod predators. Should they become a problem, consider draping the whole crop with bird netting. Netting is inexpensive and available at most garden centres or from online supply companies.

Cabbage Family

Brassicacae; cole crops

Outside of radishes, the Brassicas, or cole crop plants, are a difficult bunch for the casual square metre gardener as they require constant guarding against insect pests and are subject to club root disease. Most of the Brassicas are monster plants that are not suitable for gardens where space is a constraint. If space is a problem but cole crops are a must-have, plant them in containers fitted with drip emitters.

If space is not a factor, it's a good idea to devote an entire 3-square-metre bed to them because they require extra nitrogen in the form of lots of aged manure forked into the soil in fall, and horticultural lime in spring. Except for the radishes, all other cole crops are vegetables of considerable size, and that requires massive nutrient uptake. The horticultural lime is to raise the pH of the soil so that it is slightly alkaline. Cole crops grow best in soil with a pH of 7.2. If possible, buy, beg or borrow a soil tester so you know when to stop with the lime. Some garden centres offer free soil testing. If you can't test the soil, then fork 1.5 kg of lime into the 3-square-metre bed and it should be fine. Do not add manure and lime at the same time; they are reactive and will cancel out any benefits. Add manure, three or four bags, in fall, lime in spring, and just before planting seeds, add a good quantity of liquid organic fertilizer.

Cabbage is perhaps the most well-known Brassica.

Mustard greens are gaining in popularity.

When gardening multiple raised beds with one dedicated to cole crops, do not replant that bed with cole crops for two or three years, three being the safest. If planting cole crops with other vegetables, do not plant them in the same spot every spring; move them around and do not plant them near tomatoes, as both are nutrient and water hogs and will suffer from the competition.

Note: The main disease threat to cole crops is called club root disease, a soil fungus, and once it sets in, it's there for years. The only solution is moving the cole crops to another bed and turning the infected bed over to growing other vegetables, which will not be affected. To prevent club root infection, square metre gardeners are advised to plant seeds and not to purchase transplant seedlings, as transplants will introduce questionable soil into the garden.

Check cole crops regularly for insects, paying special attention to the under leaves, where aphids like to congregate. Pick off caterpillars, spray aphids with insecticidal soap and ring plants being munched by slugs and snails with diatomaceous earth.

Root maggots are a common threat to cole crops.

Broccoli

Brassica oleracea **var. *botrytis***

- Strictly full sun

Broccoli needs a lengthy growing season. If transplanting seedlings, figure on doing so 75–80 days before harvest, and if sowing seeds, the interminable wait will be around 100 days. Since broccoli may mature without flowering or heading when subjected to early frost in fall, it should be a spring planting vegetable for more northerly areas of Canada, while the more southerly can wait until summer. For a spring planting, start seeds indoors 6–8 weeks before transplanting after frost danger is past, or directly into the raised bed when soil temperatures reach a steady 13° C. For a later harvest, sow seeds at the beginning of summer, several days apart to prevent simultaneous maturation. Broccoli is receptive to intensive planting, say 30 cm spacing, but will yield small heads. If space is no problem, allow 40 cm of space for each plant to yield larger heads, along with side shoots.

A good companion planting for broccoli is onions, as they also like slightly alkaline soil and will be up and out long before the broccoli needs the root space.

Broccoli does well in containers, especially when drip irrigated, as it has a low tolerance for drought and will respond to that stress by refusing to head.

Harvest broccoli when the heads are about to flower, but still have tight, vibrant green buds. Use a sharp knife to cut 15 cm below the head, at an angle to prevent stem disease. After this cutting, weather and space permitting, side shoots will grow and offer another supply of sweet, succulent broccoli flowers. Cut these, and more side shoots will keep popping out until killed by a hard frost.

It seems that no matter how few plants square metre gardeners plant, or how staggered the planting, there will be a surplus. Do not fear the surplus because broccoli freezes well after blanching. To blanch, wash the head, break it into florets, and dump them into a good-sized pot of salted, boiling water for five minutes. Remove florets from boiling water and immediately place into a large bowl of ice water. Once they're cold, drain the water, set them to dry on paper towel, place into plastic freezer bags and freeze.

Best seeds: 'Purple Peacock' (purple heads) and 'White Star' (white heads).

Brussels Sprouts

Brassica oleracea var. *gemnifera*

- Tolerate partial shade

Sow seeds directly into the raised bed in midsummer for a late fall harvest; any earlier will have the plants maturing in the summer heat, resulting in malformed sprouts. Do not worry about early fall frost; this is one hardy plant, and sprouts will actually be tastier after one or two frosts. Seeds germinate quickly, usually in one week, and then the interminable wait for harvest is around 100 days. Brussels sprouts make for a good succession plant; when midsummer heat puts pay to leafy greens, pop in a few Brussels and watch them sprout, but keep in mind that they are monsters and require a minimum of 40 cm of space and plenty of additional fertilizer.

When the plant begins to mature and form sprouts, remove most leaves from the stem, leaving only the topmost leaves. Birds love Brussels sprouts, so it's a good idea to have a net cover ready should the need arise.

To harvest, just cut off the sprouts with a sharp knife and wash them in cold water. To cook, cut a cross in the hard end of each sprout, blanch in salted boiling water for five minutes, dunk them in ice water and prepare according to a favourite recipe.

If constrained by space, a container is the ticket, and why not choose a colourful variety with red sprouts?

Best seeds: 'Red Bull' (with red sprouts), 'Long Island Improved,' 'Trafalgar' and 'Bubbles.'

Cabbage

Brassica oleracea **var.** *capitata*

- Strictly full sun

Cool soil produces exceptional cabbage. If a constant supply is aimed for, use transplant seedlings for a late spring crop, then sow seeds of savoy cabbage for a summer crop because it rather likes the summer heat, then stagger plant seeds of varieties with different maturation times in late spring for harvesting during the autumn months. For spring cabbage, sow seeds indoors in late winter and transplant outdoors when all threat of frost has passed.

Just like broccoli and cauliflower, cabbage requires lots of space, fertilizer, water and 100 days to mature. There are earlier maturing varieties, but size of heads and taste is the tradeoff, so why bother. Give each plant 40 cm of space and use organic fertilizer, such as fish emulsion or kelp, every three weeks.

Cabbages are very sensitive to cold, so be prepared to cover them if there is even a hint of frost expected. When harvesting, angle-cut heads from plants to prevent rot and allow small cabbages to regrow.

Best seeds: 'Durham Early,' 'Spring Hero' and 'Greyhound' for spring varieties; 'Tundra,' 'Celtic' and 'Tarvoy' for fall varieties.

Cauliflower

Brassica oleracea var. *botrytis*

- Strictly full sun

For spring and summer harvest, sow early-maturing varieties indoors as early as February and transplant seedlings into 10 cm peat pots to get as much stem and leaf growth as possible before moving them outside once the threat of frost has passed. Cauliflower needs a head start because summer heat will have it refusing to head. For this reason, if starting seeds indoors isn't practical, cauliflower is best seeded into the raised bed in early summer for late fall harvesting. Do not worry about early frosts; the plant is hardy and can withstand several light frosts that actually serve to sweeten the flower. Plant seeds according to package instructions in well-manured and limed soil, and do not water from above.

Cauliflower matures in 80–100 days and should be harvested before the head begins to deteriorate. Cut flowers from the stem using an angle cut, and the plant will likely produce more, but smaller, flowers.

To cook a whole flower, first score the stem end and blanch in salted boiling water for eight minutes, cool in a bath of ice water and continue cooking according to a recipe. Do not blanch or cook cauliflower in aluminum pots because doing so will darken the flower.

Best seeds: 'Snowball,' 'Igloo' and 'Mayflower' for spring and summer harvest; 'Fall Giant,' 'Clapton' and 'Skywalker' for fall harvest; 'Early Snowball' and 'Late Tuscan' for self-blanching; and if coloured heads are desired, there is 'Purple Cap' and 'Violet Queen.'

Horseradish

Armoracia rusticana

- Strictly full sun

Horseradish is easy to grow but takes forever to mature, up to 150 days, and is best grown from cuttings. To obtain cuttings, shop for whole horseradish root with crown. Slice off 15 cm long, wedge-shaped sections of root starting from the crown; cuttings must have a section of crown atop each wedge of root. Plant cuttings vertically, with the crown bit up and 7.5 cm under the soil, and allow each one 45 cm of space. Horseradish does well in normal raised bed garden soil, requires no extra care and has very few insect or disease problems. Aphids can sometimes be a problem, but planting a nasturtium trap will get rid of those pests.

Horseradish is a perennial plant. When digging up the roots, leave small bits behind to start next season's crop. However, gardeners sometimes end up with more plants than they bargained for, which can be a problem if other vegetable plants share the raised bed. Horseradish is both invasive and a brute, growing to over 1 m tall with large leaves that will shade out all but the climbers. If horseradish is a must-have vegetable, say for oyster lovers, gardeners are advised to plant it in containers. On the other hand, if potatoes are going into the raised bed, a few horseradish plants will serve to keep away bugs, especially the dreaded Colorado potato beetle.

Kale

Brassica oleracea var. *acephala*

- Tolerate partial shade

Kale is a sweetheart of a garden plant and very easy to grow as long as you cool the bed with water during summer heat waves. Sow seeds in late spring when all danger of frost has passed and space seeds or transplants 30 cm apart, staggering planting times to assure a steady supply. Kale planted in cold soil will bolt early and be ruined, so make sure soil temperature is above 10° C.

Kale takes about 60 days to fully mature, but young, tender leaves can be picked anytime until the plant flowers and the leaves turn bitter. Pick leaves from the bottom of plant and not from the top so the plant may continue growing. Kale can withstand all but the hardest fall frosts, and even when frozen the leaves can still be consumed; just cook them before they thaw.

Curly kale is most popular, as the leaves are sweeter than the smooth-leafed varieties. Kale does well in containers, and its colourful leaves add pizzazz to any location.

Best seeds: 'Scarlet' and 'Redbor.'

Kohlrabi

Brassica oleracea subsp. *gongylodes*

- Tolerates partial shade

Seeds will germinate in a week, and the plants will reach maturity in 45–50 days. Gardeners who really like kohlrabi should stagger planting for a steady supply. It's easy to grow, just give each plant 25 cm of space and a little dash of horticultural lime. Do not allow kohlrabi to dry out, ever. If growing in a container, it is almost mandatory to install a drip irrigator.

Begin harvesting kohlrabi when the round stem is 5 cm in diameter. Simply cut between bulb and root with a serrated knife, and remove the leaves. Kohlrabi is usually peeled and cooked soft, but for a nice change try it peeled, sliced and mixed into a salad.

Best seeds: 'Giant Purple' and 'Purple Vienna' for purple skins; 'Giant White', 'Rapidstar' and 'White Vienna' for white skins.

Radishes

Raphanus sativus

- Tolerate partial shade

Tamest of the Brassicas, the diminutive radish is so easy and quick to grow that only the heat of summer prevents a constant supply. There are summer-maturing varieties, but these are generally small with disappointing taste. Plant seeds when soil temperature reaches 13° C (cloched beds will speed up warming). Seeds are tiny and may be dribbled into rows, then thinned out after sprouting. Germination is quick,

usually 4–5 days, with harvest available in less than a month. Stagger seeding to assure a steady supply. Radishes like plenty of water, especially in warmer weather, and do best with drip irrigation. For the largest, best-tasting radishes, plant in late summer for a late fall harvest.

To harvest radishes, pluck them from the soil and immediately sever the leafy tops with a sharp knife; otherwise the leaves will continue to draw moisture.

Best seeds: 'Cherry Belle,' 'Perfecto' and 'Crimson Giant.'

Rutabagas

Brassica napus

- Tolerate partial shade

Seeds will germinate in a week or less, but the roots will take 90–100 days to mature. Give plants 25 cm of space and don't bother to lime the soil. Time planting to coincide with fall frosts to enjoy extra-tasty roots.

Rutabagas are a Canadian hybrid, a cross between cabbage and turnip, and make very tasty fare. They can be stored in sand or sawdust in an unheated garage or cellar where temperatures approach freezing but do not fall below. For long dry storage, simply emulate commercial growers and dip the roots into melted paraffin wax to conserve moisture and maintain freshness.

> **Best seeds:** our Canadian hybridized 'Altasweet' and 'Laurentian.'

Turnips

Brassica rapa

- Tolerate partial shade

Turnips are quick to germinate and ready to dig in 40–80 days, depending on the variety. Space plants 15 cm apart and keep soil moist by daily misting or by drip irrigation. Fall turnips are much superior to early varieties, so plant in midsummer and harvest after a good hard frost, as the roots will be more flavourful. Harvest when roots are more than 5 cm in diameter and take care not to cut or bruise the roots; any root damage will cut into storage time.

Turnips may be stored for several months in a cold, dark, humid cellar. Or, after a hard frost, just pull out the roots, cut off the leaves, lay the turnips on the soil and cover with a mulch, such as raked-up leaves. "X" marks the spot, because you don't want to be feeling around for turnip roots in a snowdrift.

> **Best seeds:** 'White Knight', 'Golden Ball' and the U.S. heirloom 'Gilfeather.'

Carrot Family

Apiaceae

The following (with the exception of fennel) are the best plants in the carrot family for raised bed culture. Other members of the carrot family that may be grown in pots or containers include anise, lovage, coriander, cumin and dill.

Carrots

Daucus carota

- Tolerate partial shade

Carrots are a perfect vegetable for 3-square-metre raised beds, especially deep beds. They are also a fun crop in that gardeners can play them like an accordion. Squeezing them together, say with only 2.5 cm of space, will yield petites; give them 5 cm, and regular sized carrots will spring from the soil. But give them each 30 cm of leeway, and they'll be giant sized, the world record holder weighing in at 8.61 kg (18.985 lb.).

> **Best seeds:** the early 'Parano' and 'Sugarsnax,' or the coloured 'Purple Haze.'

Celery

Apium graveolens **var.** *dulce*

- Strictly full sun

While technically a cool crop, celery has the irritating habit of bolting (going to flower) if nighttime temperatures dip below 13° C. Celery is a perfect raised bed crop, but it is a pig for water and nutrients and must be amply supplied with both, the latter in the form of liquid fish emulsion applied sparingly, but often. Seeds or transplants must be in the ground only after nighttime temperatures rise above 13° C and spaced 20 cm apart. That doesn't sound intensive, but giving them less will result in tough, stringy stalks.

If gardeners want exceptionally tender celery stalks, they must emulate commercial growers and blanch the stalks, which involves boxing the bottom portion of the plants and allowing sunshine to reach only the topmost leaves. Blanching can be done with thin boards, waxed cardboard or any opaque material that won't go soggy from contact with soil. Or, gardeners may plant a celery hybrid called 'Golden Self-Blanching' that, if planted in a block, will self-blanch the inner plant stalks.

Celery matures around 90 days, but separate stalks can be cut from the base after 30–35 days, leaving the plant to regrow. Celery can withstand light frosts at the end of the growing season. After harvest, store it by uprooting plants and placing them upright in a cold place and covering the roots with moist sand.

> **Best seeds:** 'Monterey,' 'Giant Pink' and 'Pascal.' For self-blanching, either 'Tango' or 'Victoria.'

Celeriac

Apium graveolens **var.** *rapaceum*

- Strictly full sun

This is a variety of celery grown for the culinary attributes of its knobby, turnip-like root. Seeds germinate in 2–3 weeks and then it's 120 days to maturity, but celeriac is very disease and bug resistant and requires no special care other than extra water during heat waves. The peeled root can be julienned for salads (tastes like Waldorf salad), cubed and boiled as a side dish, melon-balled and sautéed with butter, or grated and used to make the culinary eye-opener that is celery salt.

To make celery salt, grate (use the large holes in a box grater) 0.5 kg peeled celeriac into 750 mL sea salt and mix thoroughly. Place the mixture into an airtight container and refrigerate for a few days to allow the celery flavour to permeate the salt. Spread the mixture onto a baking tray and bake in 95° C (200° F) oven until completely dry (2–3 hours). Run dried mixture through a spice grinder and store in an airtight container. Celery salt adds pizzazz to almost any food and is especially good sprinkled on steamed and buttered vegetables.

Fennel

Foeniculum vulgare

- Strictly full sun

Fennel is best planted in containers because its roots exude chemicals that inhibit growth in many vegetable plants. It is easy to grow; just allow 15 cm between plants and make sure the soil is well turned with perlite and extra compost for good drainage. Fennel will forgive the odd parching, but not in midsummer. Seeds germinate in two weeks, and plants mature in two months, during which time they may grow to over 90 cm tall.

There are two popular varieties: common garden fennel, which is grown for its flavourful seeds and leaves, and Florence fennel (also called finocchio), which is grown for its stalk and bulb and used in salads or cooked as a side dish. Florence fennel may be blanched by either mounding soil around the stem or fitting plants with paper collars about two weeks before maturity. If seeds are the intended crop, gardeners will have to overwinter the roots because the plant only produces seeds at the end of the second season. Gently fork up the roots, clean them off and store them in moist—never soaked or dried out—sand.

Note: Do not plant fennel near dill, as the two are too closely related and will cross-pollinate, ruining both.

Parsley

Petroselinum crispum

- Tolerates partial shade

Parsley seeds need a long germination period of about a month, so they are best started indoors and transplanted as seedlings. Parsley is well behaved in raised beds, where it appreciates well-draining soil with plenty of organic matter and high nutrient levels.

When harvesting parsley, cut stems at the base to stimulate a lush regrowth. In late fall, a few plants should be dug up, replanted in pots and brought inside. Parsley varieties are either flat-leaf or curly, and both types dry and freeze well. To use parsley strictly as an herb garnish is a big mistake; those dark green leaves are loaded with vitamins A, C and K along with a host of antioxidants. Throwing a bunch into a smoothie could save someone's life, but that someone served parsley fried in clarified butter will think they've already died and gone to heaven.

Parsnips

Pastinaca sativa

- Strictly full sun

Seeds take up to three weeks to germinate, so parsnips are best started early inside and transplanted outside. Plant seeds 1 cm deep and cover with sifted soil or compost. Not all seeds will germinate, so plant extras and thin after they emerge.

Parsnips appreciate raised bed culture and will reward growers with a taste treat and a change of attitude. They grow best in deep raised beds. Leave them in the ground and they may be dug from late fall through winter if the bed is protected by a cloche or deep mulch of straw.

Leafy Greens

Asteraceae, Amaranthaceae

Endive

Cichorium endivia

- Strictly full sun

Belgium endive, that compact, bullet-shaped, tight-leafed vegetable found in the produce section of food markets, is a biennial plant (two years to harvest) and is not recommended for space- and time-constrained gardeners. Annual endives are the vegetable plants for square metre gardeners. They are as easy to grow as lettuce and come in two varieties: curly endive, or frisee lettuce, and the broad-leafed escarole.

Endive is great for intercropping, but start seeds indoors 6–7 weeks before the anticipated last frost and set out immediately after frost danger has passed, as the first heat of summer will cause the plants to bolt. For an extended fall crop, stagger-sow seeds every two weeks beginning mid-July and thin after sprouting to allow for 40 cm of space between plants. Do not scrimp on space with these guys because leaf-touching may cause plants to rot.

Lettuce

Letuca sativa

- Tolerates partial shade

Lettuce is easy to grow and surprisingly hardy for such a delicate-looking plant. There are three popular varieties—head (iceberg), leaf (bibb) and romaine—

with all being good for successive planting. Sow seeds early and successively every week until summer, and then start again in midsummer for fall harvesting. Lettuce will bolt in summer heat; however, if gardeners are using drip irrigation and have cloche hoops installed, then shade cloth will enable the cultivation of lettuce from early spring to winter, with the romaine variety able to withstand several frosts.

Planting half a 3-square-metre raised bed in lettuce will produce around 60 heads. Plant seeds according to package directions, paying special attention to depth and covering; lettuce seeds require light to germinate and should be covered with a very thin layer of sifted soil or none at all. Seeds take 1–2 weeks to germinate and should be misted daily until sprouted. If transplanting

seedlings, allow leaf and romaine varieties 13 cm of space and head lettuce 25 cm; if seeding directly, thin sprouts to the same spacing.

Head lettuce matures in 70–80 days, leaf lettuce about 40 days, and romaine 60–65 days. Harvest leaf lettuce in early mornings when it is still dewy, and remove only outer leaves, allowing the inner leaves to continue growing. If whole heads are desired, cut tops with a sharp knife, leaving 5 cm of stalk to grow new leaves.

Radicchio

Cichorium intybus

- Strictly full sun

This vegetable looks like a small red and white cabbage, but it is not a relative. Sow seeds indoors 6–8 weeks before you plan to transplant it outside. Radicchio seeds are extremely tiny and should be mixed with a small amount of dry sand and the mixture broadcast onto a prepared surface. Then cover with a thin layer of sifted soil and mist with water daily. After seedlings emerge, usually in 1–2 weeks, thin to 5 cm and

keep misting. Follow this procedure if sowing outdoors, and thin seedlings to 25 cm apart.

Radicchio is at its best when planted for a fall harvest, but seeds will often fail to germinate outdoors in the heat of summer, so they are best sprouted indoors in a cool place. Do not water radicchio plants from above or spray with water, as doing so will cause leaf and crown rot.

Salsify

Tragopogon porrifolius

- Tolerates partial shade

Some people call salsify "oyster plant" because it has a taste similar to oysters, with a touch of artichoke. It is a root vegetable that looks like a parsnip. It takes forever to mature, up to 130 days, but is very easy to grow. Plant according to package instructions, allowing 2–3 weeks for seed germination and an interminable four months until harvest. A few light frosts before harvest will improve its flavour. Salsify is fairly disease- and bug-resistant and needs no special attention other than extra water during hot spells.

Gardeners thinking 130 days a long wait will be doubly frustrated when it comes to cooking salsify, as it takes more than an hour of boiling to soften. Peel roots and immediately drop them into a bath of vinegar or lemon juice and water to keep them from darkening, then boil until tender. Use them as you would potatoes or turnips.

Spinach

Spinacia oleracea

- Full sun, but likes shading from noonday sun

Plant seeds early, and when they've sprouted (7–10 days), plant more and keep planting more until late spring. Plants will bolt in summer heat, so lay off planting any more until midsummer. Spinach needs 13 cm of space and lots of water. When grown successively, plants require additional liquid organic fertilizer, such as fish emulsion. Spinach is good for intercropping with tomatoes and should be watched for cabbage loopers and aphids.

Spinach is ready to harvest when the plant has grown more than six large leaves (about 40 days). Each planting should be used within two weeks because the leaves tend to toughen. Use baby leaves raw in salads, and cook the larger leaves for dinner sides. Cook only in water left on leaves from washing, and do not cook in iron or aluminum pots, as the metal will impart a metallic taste.

Swiss Chard

Beta vulgaris subsp. *cicla*

- Tolerates partial shade

Direct sow Swiss chard in the raised bed 15 cm apart. Seeds will germinate in 8–12 days with plants reaching maturity in 60 days, but small, tender leaves can be cut after 30 days, leaving the plant to grow more.

This is one hardy plant that will sail through hot summers with flags flying. However, if the flags get too high, they'll become tough and inedible. Cutting the leaves 5 cm above the crown will produce new baby leaves that are great in salads. Or cook chard like spinach, using only the water that adheres to the leaves after washing. Do not use salt, as it toughens the leaves.

Onion Family

Alliaceae

An onion can make people cry, but there's never been a vegetable that can make people laugh.

–Will Rogers, humourist

Bulb Onions

Allium cepa; A. fistulosum

- Strictly full sun

Onions are perfect for intercropping; get seeds or transplants into the soil as early as possible and they'll be up and out while other vegetable plants are just getting started. They also make a good succession crop; get one batch out and plant another.

There are three categories of onions— short day, long day and intermediate— with each channelling energy to bulbs

according to the number of hours of daylight. Gardeners with cloches or microclimates, or who are in the most southerly areas of Canada, are able to support any of the three, but the category most favoured and successful is the long day, such as 'Pontiac.' Plant seeds according to package instructions

(usually 5 cm deep), and allow transplants about 7.5 cm of space between plants. Tiny onion bulbs called "sets" are popular with row gardeners because they can be planted in fall and be ready for harvest in early spring, but they are not recommended for raised bed gardeners because their planting interferes with fall soil preparation and may attract winter-starved grey squirrels.

Growing onions from seed to mature bulb will take 110–120 days; transplants will need 80–90 days, and sets 60 days. Onions may be harvested at any time for green onions or shallots, but if mature bulbs are wanted, wait until half the plants have fallen tops; then gently push down the tops of those remaining upright and allow them to dry in the sunshine for a few days before gently digging out the bulbs. Pick a sunny, breezy day to dig onion bulbs, and allow

them a few days outside to air dry. To cure onions for long keeping, move them to a warm, well-ventilated, dry place and allow the bulbs to sit until the necks are thoroughly dry, usually around two weeks. Store cured onions in a cool, dry place in a mesh bag or by braiding the tops.

The main threat to a quality onion crop is "bolting," and no, they won't be running away; they'll be switching into reproductive mode by channelling energy from leaves to flowers, usually in response to the stress of over-heated soil. Gardeners should take precautions if a spell of hot weather is predicted and lay on extra waterings to cool the soil. If using greenhouse fabric, get it onto the hoops for the duration of the hot spell. Finding some flowers on your onion crop is no need to panic; simply snip them off to prevent splitting and mark the plants for early harvest and immediate consumption.

Onion bulbs can be different colours, usually white, red or yellow, and contain less or more sugar depending on the variety. Dry onions have a low moisture content and are high in sulphur, two attributes that enable long storage under proper conditions. Dry onions with higher sugar content are called sweet onions and should be consumed quickly because they do not store as well.

> **Tip:** When pulling onions, use a small hand fork; it is easier on both onions and gardeners.

- Yellow onion, or storage onion: The most popular of the dry onions; the sugar content and volatile compounds are well balanced and lend themselves to countless culinary applications.

- White onion, or paper onion: This is another common cooking onion pulled from the ground as paper-covered bulbs after the shoots have begun to wither. These onions contain less sulphur than yellow onions and have a cleaner, sharper flavour.

- Red onion, or Italian onion: These are dry onions with a high sugar content that permits consuming raw in salads or as burger toppings.

- Spanish onion: These are large yellow onions with a high sugar content that enables raw consumption in salads or as burger toppings. These onions do not store well and should be consumed immediately after harvest.

- Sweet onion, or spring onion: Sweet onions, like the famous 'Vidalia' or 'Walla Walla' varieties, are harvested in spring or summer and consumed immediately because they contain more water and sugar than dry onions and do not store well.

- Scallion and green onion: Scallions are simply bulb onions picked before maturity and usually from slightly different varieties, but any onion can be a scallion. Simply plant as early in spring as possible, and after the shoots have grown to 20 cm tall, dig them up and voila—green onion tops and scallion bottoms.

Chives

Allium schoenoprasum

- Strictly full sun

Chives are a culinary necessity; no chef can get along without a supply. Chives are perennial plants grown from either bulbs or seeds. They like containers, any size, and will do well as long as they have full sun, rich soil and adequate water. In late spring, the plant produces purple flowers that, for culinary purposes, should be removed because they interfere with shoot growth. Harvest chives with sharp scissors. Snip, snip, and it's onto the bagels and cream cheese.

Egyptian Walking Onion

Allium x *proliferum*

- Strictly full sun

Also known as tree onion, Egyptian walking onion is a perennial top-setting onion that produces bulblets rather than flowers. As the plant grows, the bulblets weigh the top down to soil level, where a new plant is formed and the process repeated. This plant literally walks about, which is perhaps not a good idea for a well-planned raised bed garden. It does have a few attributes; it tastes great and is one of the hardiest plants around. Walking onions are the first up in spring and the last to go in fall.

Garlic

Allium sativum

- Strictly full sun

Garlic is the prince of the onion family, but because it takes forever to mature, up to 150 days, and is a bit difficult for even experienced gardeners, it is probably best to purchase it at farmers' markets. If garlic is a must-have, then gardeners should purchase the finest-looking garlic bulbs they can find at a food market, break them up into cloves and plant the cloves. Only the biggest and best cloves will do. Plant them 5 cm deep with the pointy end up. They should sprout in 10–12 days, and if not, well, the bulbs were probably from China and irradiated.

Garlic is fairly bug proof, and with its only demand being water, it can very easily become forgetzees; "X" marks the spot is a must-do endeavour. Gardeners might mark down the following: "See you in five months, garlic."

> **Tip:** When buying garlic bulbs for planting purposes, make sure of the bulb's origin: "Gee Martha, it's been three weeks and no garlic sprouts. The Egyptian walking onions have run off and the raised bed smells rotten. I wonder why?"

Leeks

Allium ampeloprasum

- Tolerate partial shade

The ultimate slow food garden is a 3-square-metre raised bed planted in nothing but leeks, garlic and horseradish. This princess of the onion family is easy to grow, mild in flavour and has many culinary applications, but it takes up to 150 days to reach maturity. For that reason, leek is not a recommended vegetable plant for square metre gardeners with space constraints (it's a thumb twiddler). However, if leeks are a must-have vegetable, or gardeners want them less than mature (think scallions), plant them east of climbing plants so they get only half a day's sun, and water liberally. The long growing period is exhausting, so leeks will appreciate a monthly snack of liquid organic fertilizer.

If long, white stems are wanted, gardeners will have to start hilling up soil when the plants are 10 cm tall. Hilling up is simply the careful mounding of soil around the stalk to block sunlight—the same technique employed to produce white asparagus.

Squash Family

Cucurbitaceae; cucurbits

Repeating crops in the same raised bed is not a good idea, and this is especially true with the cucurbit family of plants, for which a small problem with plant disease will return the next season as a very large problem. All members of the cucurbit family require full sun for optimum growth, and all standard varieties are monoecious, meaning the plants produce both male and female flowers, with the fruit forming behind the female flowers.

> **Tip:** To control moulds and fungus diseases of cucurbits, always water plants from below. A drip irrigation system and timer works best for this plant family.

Cucumbers

Cucumis sativus

Cucumbers are available in both vine and bush varieties, with the former being the choice of square metre gardeners because they permit intercropping. Cucumber plants are extremely cold sensitive and should be started early indoors or sown outdoors when all threat of frost has passed and soil temperature is above 15° C. Cucumbers do well in containers; just make sure there is adequate drainage and plenty of space between the soil surface and pot rim for plenty of water. No matter where they're planted, they require a trellis or fence to climb.

In addition to fungal infections, squash borers can threaten various cucurbits.

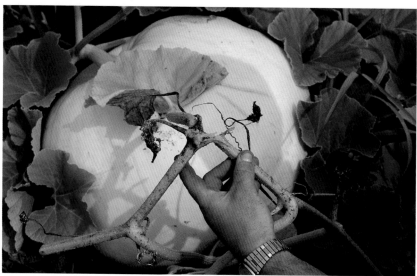

Cucumbers are easy to grow, but they are targets for various viral and bacterial diseases. To control these diseases avoid repetitive planting, water from below or employ a drip irrigation system, keep soil weed free and check under leaves for bugs (both bugs and weeds transmit viral and bacterial diseases), remove singular infected plants, and do not pick cukes when plants are wet from morning dew, as doing so will spread minor infections.

Best seeds: 'Masterpiece,' 'Cucumber Dixie,' 'Marketmore 76' and dozens of heirloom varieties such as 'Boothby's Blonde' and 'Double Yield.' For pickling gherkins, gardeners may either harvest immature cukes or try specially bred varieties, such as 'National Pickling' or 'Pioneer.'

Melons

Cucumis melo

Melons are field crops, and unless an entire bed is dedicated to their cultivation, such as a long, 60 cm wide bed constructed next to a sunny wall or fence, forget about including them in the raised bed gang. If yard space is no constraint and a composter is in action or in the planning stages, grow melons there; they will embrace it with vines and leaves and make it look interesting.

Squash

Cucurbita pepo

The trouble is, you cannot grow just one zucchini. Minutes after you plant a single seed, hundreds of zucchini will barge out of the ground and sprawl around the garden, menacing the other vegetables.

–Dave Barry, humour columnist

Zucchini: These are easy to grow, but very sensitive to cold, so hold off transplanting or sowing seeds outside until all danger of frost is passed and soil temperature is at or above 15° C. Sow seeds 2.5 cm deep and three to a spot, thinning to the strongest one after sprouting—usually one week. Because the plant is monoecious and a hog for space, one plant trained onto a trellis is advisable; even one will provide fruit almost as fast as it can be harvested. If the garden is tiny, hand pollination is advised: strip the petals from picked male flowers (those with no fruit beginning behind) and dab the female stigma (the raised portion within the female flower) with the pollen-coated male anther. These guys are big feeders, so pile on the compost and be liberal with the liquid organic fertilizer—and don't forget that the unnecessary male flowers have culinary uses.

Marrow: This is another summer squash that, while extremely popular in Europe, failed to make the produce hit parade in Canada, probably because after cooking it tastes similar to zucchini. In fact, marrow squash are actually just bigger zucchini, and everything about them is similar, including cultivation—sow seeds or transplant into warm, moisture-retentive soil, give them something to climb, protect them from cold, pile on the nutrients and do not water from above. Those gardeners feeling the urge to plant marrow should confine themselves to one plant; even one will supply the entire neighbourhood.

> **Best seeds:** 'Spineless Beauty,' 'Dark Green' and 'Gold Rush.'

Pumpkin: For gardeners not experienced in the joys and terrors of parenthood, growing pumpkins will provide a fair preview. Pumpkin plants whine, cry, throw tantrums and are constantly coming down with something. But then the kids are suddenly grown up, graduating from college and making the parents very proud. All hail the great pumpkin: infuriating, rewarding and not for a standard raised bed.

Gardeners with a sunny fence or wall (at least six hours) who cannot live without the kid experience are advised to tack up a trellis and train small varieties of pumpkin plants to climb, employing net slings to hold the fruits. If no sunny fence is available, or it's being used for other climbers, then plant either regular or small varieties of pumpkins around a composter. Simply dig a hole, fill it with raised bed soil amended with plenty of compost and aged manure, and make a mound 15 cm high. For multiple plants, allow plenty of space between the mounds and plant three seeds 2.5 cm deep and equidistant from each other, thinning to the single strongest when sprouts emerge. Plant in late spring or early summer, as a mere touch of frost will kill them. Seed germination is 7–10 days, full maturity is 90–100 days, and in between, gardeners must cater to their every whim, which is mostly lots of liquid organic fertilizer and water, but not cold water—warm, like from a sitting hose. Inspect daily for bugs, diseases and moulds and do not water from above.

Ditto for other winter squash.

Tomato Family

Solanaceae

The most infamous member of this family of plants is the very poisonous *Atropa belladonna*, commonly called deadly nightshade. This association reflected on the innocent tomato well into the 19th century, with many people believing the consumption of tomatoes was a dangerous undertaking. The notion of danger was reinforced by the tomato's former scientific name, *Solanum lycopersicum*, which means "wolf apple." Wolf apple refers to a group of plants used to poison wolves, such as monkshood, wolfbane and mandrake.

Tomatoes used to be feared poisonous; monkshood (below) really is poisonous.

Eggplants

Solanum melongena

- Strictly full sun

Eggplants, also called aubergines, are not the easiest vegetable to grow; loved by almost every bug on the planet and a major target of plant diseases, the plants also take up a lot of space and are high maintenance. Eggplants are available in many varieties and all the colours of the rainbow, but the most popular with both gardeners and cooks is the Western, a plant sporting the familiar oval shaped, purple-skinned produce.

Eggplants do not appreciate cold spring nights and must be started indoors and transplanted to the garden only when

nighttime temperatures hold steady above 13° C. Seeds germinate in 1–2 weeks. If keeping seedlings under fluorescent lights, place them close to the lights to deter them from becoming leggy; if keeping them on a windowsill, get into the habit of turning the pots or tray daily so all sides get equal light.

Eggplants require 60 cm of space, along with a support device such as a trellis or spare tomato cage. Common diseases include blossom end rot, which also affects other members of the spud family, so avoid planting eggplant anywhere its relatives have been the previous two seasons. Mature eggplants will not tolerate a fall frost, so be prepared to cloche or cover the crop with plastic sheeting.

The plant matures in an interminable 120–140 days. Harvest the fruit when it reaches a diameter of 10 cm. It should be consumed shortly after harvesting because it does not keep well, even when refrigerated.

Peppers

Capsicum annuum

- Strictly full sun

Peppers are another cold-sensitive crop that must be started indoors for transplant when frost danger has long passed and nighttime temperatures are holding steady above 13° C. The most common pepper varieties are bell, banana, Italian and cherry peppers. Bell peppers may be yellow, orange, red or even purple, with the common green being an unripe coloured variety.

Seeds germinate in three weeks (quicker when soaked) and do not appreciate root disturbance during transplanting, so take great care when setting them out. Space them 20–25 cm apart in

raised beds, and be prepared to cloche or cover with plastic sheeting should nighttime temperatures take a plunge. Stake plants when they become tall and supply them with plenty of liquid organic fertilizer, such as kelp or fish emulsion.

Fruits mature around 80 days, but may be harvested anytime after 60 days depending on preferred ripeness. To harvest peppers green, wait until the skin turns waxy and shiny. Peppers will not keep for long periods and are best consumed shortly after picking.

Peppers do well in containers. They need a fair amount of attention, but the container can be moved around throughout the season to take advantage of hot spots.

Potatoes

Solanum tuberosum

- Strictly full sun

Seeds may be started indoors and the seedlings transplanted after frost danger has passed. Seeds germinate in two weeks, and transplants require 25 cm of space. Another option is to plant old potatoes with sprouting eyes. Cut them so that each cut section has one or two eyes, and air dry them before planting to prevent rotting. Gardeners may also plant those small seed potatoes sold as "new potatoes" in the produce sections of most food markets. Each cut section or seed potato needs a hole 15 cm deep. If planting lots, simply make a trench, lay in a section every 25 cm and then fill in the trench.

To prevent sunlight from reaching developing potatoes and turning them green and inedible, gardeners must begin hilling up plants or shoots with soil, keeping only the top 15 cm of stem above ground. Figure on 120 days to maturity, but small potatoes can be dug up anytime after 60 days; simply tunnel under the plant with a hand and grab what you need.

Potato plants are the favourite food of several insect species and must be watched carefully. For this reason and for ease of harvesting, it is advisable to employ a potato box when growing spuds (see p. 54). One 1.2 m by 1.2 m potato box will yield about 45 kg (100 lb) of mature spuds, but with most gardeners digging them up as small or intermediate-sized spuds, yields are generally around 20 kg.

Tomatoes

Lycopersicon lycopersicum

- Strictly full sun

There are hundreds of tomato cultivars, but only two types: determinates, meaning all the fruit ripens in unison; and indeterminates, meaning there are luscious, ripe and ripening tomatoes on the vines from maturity to late fall. Both varieties are popular, the determinate with sauce and paste canners and the indeterminate for after the canners run out. However, the determinate plant is a bush, which somewhat cripples intercropping; square metre gardeners constrained by space are advised to stick with the indeterminate climbers.

Tomato plants are not especially hardy and will succumb to frost, so avoid the temptation to seed or transplant until late spring, when nighttime temperatures hold steady above 13° C. Many gardeners buy started tomato plants at markets, but starting tomatoes indoors

is a snap. Simply pre-germinate seeds to weed out the duds: sprinkle seeds onto a layer of wet, but not soggy paper towel, enclose the towel in a covered container (if planting different cultivars do not forget to write the name on the container to prevent forgetzees) and place it in a warm spot, checking daily for moisture. After seeds sprout, transfer them to soil in prepared cells and trays, or any small container, but don't forget to add drainage holes.

Starting seeds indoors will allow gardeners a head start, but surprisingly not that much, as seeds planted directly into raised beds catch up very quickly. One way to truly get a head start is to employ a cloche, covering the transplants whenever temperatures dip below 10° C. Tomato plants are big feeders but should only be fertilized after the flowers have

plants also require something to climb on—a stake, cage, trellis or fence. They will need tying onto the supports as they grow (tie them loosely with twine, strips of soft rag or sections of pantyhose).

Seeds planted directly in the raised bed will germinate in about eight days and reach maturity around 90–100 days; figure 40 days from flower to fruit. Vine-ripened tomatoes should be consumed within a few days of picking and kept at room temperature. Do not refrigerate tomatoes, as it will adversely affect texture and flavour.

set; any earlier will promote leaf growth and delay fruiting. Tomato plants love phosphorus, so dig in some bone meal and extra compost before seeding or transplanting. Indeterminate tomato

Tip: Tomatoes naturally issue a ripening gas called ethylene: the same gas used by shippers to ripen immature tomatoes while on their way to market. Many other fruits issue ethylene gas, including bananas, apples, avocados and pears, and these will hasten the ripening of each other and ethylene-sensitive leafy vegetables if stored in close proximity.

Growing Big Tomatoes

Getting the kids in on the cultivar selection is fun and could be profitable; tomato growing contests have become popular, with the biggest tomato to date weighing 3.6 kg (8 lb). There is not a kid on the planet, or adult for that matter, who would not love growing a giant tomato; here's the skinny on how it's done.

Select a cultivar that produces big tomatoes, such as 'Big Boy,' 'Better Boy,' 'Beefmaster,' 'Whopper' or 'Supersteak,' and plant two of them equidistant from each other in a 3-square-metre bed fitted out with a drip irrigator and fertilizer injector. Use an expandable or tall tomato cage around each plant. As the plants grow, start feeding them with liquid organic fertilizer once a week until they are 60 cm tall, then begin feeding twice a week. Pruning is also important. Remove all lower branches to 50 cm above ground, and remove all suckers, but not leaves. After a few tomatoes have formed, choose three or four on the lowest branches and pinch off all others and flowers. After a few weeks, the gardener can select the "biggie" and cut off the rest. Do not allow any more blossoms, suckers or fruit, just pinch them all off and watch the fun happen.

Note: If space is no constraint, square metre gardeners could set aside a bed to grow different giant vegetables every season. Giant vegetables are fun and educational for kids and are the central attraction at barbecue parties.

Growing Tomatoes in Containers

All tomato plants do nicely in containers; just keep in mind that big tomato plants have big roots that require big containers, while smaller cultivars and cherry tomatoes will be happy in smaller vessels. Also keep in mind that smaller containers require extra watering, sometimes twice a day. Terracotta pots are too porous and generally unsuitable for tomatoes unless a drip emitter is installed.

Both determinate and indeterminate types can be raised in containers, and a very neat method to do this is to select containers that will accommodate tomato cages—squat cages for the determinates and taller ones for the indeterminates. A good soil mix for container tomato plants is half raised bed soil and half compost, which will help retain water. Water retention and size are the prime considerations when selecting containers for tomatoes, but there is also weight, and if any movement of large containers is required, wheeled platforms are recommended.

Pruning Tomato Plants

Left on its own, a tomato plant will double in size every two weeks until it becomes an unsightly mass of stems and leaves. Leaves make the sugar necessary to produce large, ripe tomatoes and shield the tomatoes from the hot sun, but too many leaves will not only provide a home for moulds and other disease, but also shade out too much sunshine, reducing sugar production for fruiting.

Tomato plants have one main stem but will quickly become multi-stemmed from the node above first fruit, second fruit and so forth. More stems mean more fruit of a smaller size and a much larger plant. Gardeners overly constrained by space or who are growing tomato plants in containers are advised

to keep only the main stem tied loosely to a single stake, while those employing cages in raised beds can allow three or four stems. Suckers are any side shoots not destined to become a branch that emerge from the crotch between the main stem and branches, and these must be removed by pinching off with thumb and forefinger. As tomato plants grow taller, bottom leaves loose importance as sugar producers and will begin to turn yellow; remove these leaves by pinching or with pruning shears, remembering to disinfect shears with alcohol or bleach afterward.

Heirloom Tomatoes

Most tomatoes purchased at food markets are genetically modified to facilitate machine harvesting and for disease resistance, with taste and texture a minor concern. These commercial tomatoes are so far removed from those harvested by square metre gardeners that it might be funny if not for the fact that most of today's young people believe the commercial tomato to be the real thing. Gardeners with children are strongly advised to be present when the kids get their first taste of a real garden tomato.

Canada has a proud history of hybridizing tomatoes with exceptional taste that are better able to deal with our climate. During the late-19th and 20th centuries, Canadian Department of Agriculture breeding stations, commercial and private breeders and home gardeners released over 100 distinctly Canadian tomatoes for commercial and home

cultivation. A lot of love went into breeding and growing those tomatoes, but for commercial cultivators, picking them was too labour intensive and some thought was given to developing a mechanized picker. It was called the Blackwelder tomato harvester, and it worked like a dream save for squishing the tomatoes. The machine needed tougher tomatoes, and after a little more thought, a California crop scientist named Jack Hanna came up with the ancestor of the tasteless, commercially grown fruit that today's produce managers fob off as tomatoes. Machines soon took over the entire spectrum of tomato culture—they planted, picked and packed, and all so cheaply that produce buyers forgot about our wonderful

Canadian tomatoes. Many of the varieties just disappeared, but many were saved by thoughtful gardeners and organizations such as Seeds of Diversity.

Canadians consume about 40 kg of gene-fiddled tomatoes per annum— a startling amount, but even more startling is that, according to polls, half of the produce-buying public has given up on commercial tomatoes and has elected to either buy at farmers' markets or grow their own. The home-growing of tomatoes has become a national mania, prompting greenhouse growers to go full-out in winter in anticipation of the great spring buying binge of everything from seedlings to half-grown potted plants, most of which are genetically altered varieties for early fruiting and disease resistance.

Most home gardeners buy what is offered and are generally happy with the results. Square metre gardeners are by nature adventurous and willing to gamble, and for them there is the challenge of growing almost extirpated heritage tomatoes of exceptional quality and taste. Unlike the commonly retailed packaged seeds and started plants, heirloom tomatoes have not been bred to resist bugs and disease, so they require due diligence on the part of gardeners. However, the end result is all tomato, a taste revelation, and because they are open pollinator varieties, gardeners can save seeds and expect a duplicate crop next season. Dozens of Canadian companies sell heirloom tomato seeds; a list is available online at Seeds of Diversity.

Other Popular Vegetables

Corn

Zea mays

Who doesn't like fresh sweet corn, but unless you have a community garden allotment or a huge backyard, it makes no sense to grow it. Corn takes up too much space and requires too much attention and at harvest time delivers up a measly one or two ears on every stalk. Purchase fresh corn at farmers' markets and look for varieties such as 'Golden Bantam' or 'Seneca Chief' that were family favourites before the genetically modified sugar sweets came along—the yellow corn: "Gee Martha, this yellow corn is great. It actually tastes like corn and not sugar pops."

Rhubarb

Rheum rhabarbarum

Rhubarb is a must-have plant for some gardeners, but probably is not the best choice for raised bed gardens with space constraints. A wiser alternative to raised bed planting is a sunny corner where the soil can be dug out, replaced with bedding soil and the plant left to mature. Rhubarb is a perennial plant and requires one or two seasons of maturing before any stems can be harvested. Rhubarb requires very little attention but appreciates a liberal application of fertilizer and compost in early spring. Harvest stems when they are 2.5 cm wide, and use the poisonous leaves to concoct a very effective insecticide (see p. 129).

Sorrel

Rumex acetosa

Sorrel is a close relative of rhubarb and a much-overlooked garden plant that is perfect for raised bed culture. Unlike its relative rhubarb, the leaves of sorrel may be consumed, with their tart, lemony flavour finding many culinary uses. Sow seeds early and protect the seedlings from frost with a cloche or floating cover. Time is a constraint with sorrel because the first waves of summer heat will turn the leaves bitter. Plant seeds in full sun and allow at least 13 cm of space.

Sunchoke

Helianthus tuberosus

Also known as Jerusalem artichoke, the sunchoke is a close relative of the common sunflower. It is a must-have plant for gardeners suffering from diabetes because the tubers make an ideal replacement for potatoes; during cooking, sunchoke's carbohydrates break down into fructose rather than glucose. Be warned, sunchoke is a space hog and may reach heights of almost 2 m, but it will pay its way by sporting lots of yellow flowers. Plant tubers 10 cm deep, allowing 90 cm of space, and only harvest tubers after the first fall frost (do so carefully because the tubers have very thin skins).

The Herbs

The garden is the poor man's apothecary.

–German proverb

Herbs were the first medicines, and those plants have been the darlings of gardeners since the dawn of civilization. Mesopotamian burial sites dating back 50,000 years contain medicinal herbs. Chinese herbal records date back over 5000 years, early Egyptian pharoahs had herbs placed in their tombs and pyramids, India has a long history of herbal medicine, and both the ancient Greeks and Romans depended on herbalists to cure their ills. During the Middle Ages, ordinary people discovered that herbs growing wild in the countryside added pizzazz to food. Free for the taking, culinary herbs quickly became indispensable in regional cuisines: chives, garlic, dill and especially members of the wild and woolly mint family.

> **Note:** Because kitchen garden herbs will be accessed continuously, it is best to locate them as close to the kitchen as possible. If growing in raised beds, consider a parterre—a small, raised divided bed exclusively for herbs—or use containers and pots of various sizes to add interest to the patio.

Herbs are easy to grow, useful and delicious.

Mint Family

Lamiaceae

The mints are a happy go lucky, independent family of plants that will place few demands on growers outside of six to eight hours of sun, adequate water and well-draining soil. Affording too much TLC to any of the mints will usually have a detrimental effect, so do not fertilize and avoid overwatering.

Keep them confined because they are extremely gregarious and will want to spread everywhere. Do not plant mints in large raised vegetable beds; instead use containers, and place them close to the kitchen door for convenience. Do not allow the plants to go to flower. Snip off flowers before they get started and the herbs will usually return to growing leaves.

All of the mints are prolific and ideal for containers.

Basil

Ocimum basilicum

Basil was considered a purely medicinal herb until the tomato arrived in Europe. When cooks discovered the amazing culinary relationship, they began to cultivate both in earnest. All gardeners need is a medium-sized container. Basil is a prodigious grower and will keep the kitchen supplied all summer. Rumours abound that basil is difficult, but that is hooey; the plant is easy as long you meet its requirements—fertile, well-drained soil, seven hours of sunshine and protection from cold.

Lavender

Lavandula spp.

Nothing energizes the spirit like the rich aroma of lavender. Lavender stems and flowers contain glands that secrete the fragrant oil with so many uses: soap, potpourri to scent linen closets, bath oil and flavouring for candy, meats, stews, jams and jellies. The plant is easy to grow, but like all members of the mint family it can become invasive and is best confined in containers, a parterre, a small raised bed or a divided raised bed shared by several herb species.

Marjoram

Origanum majorana

Marjoram is a culinary herb similar in taste to oregano, but sweeter. Sensitive to cold, marjoram should be planted when there is no danger of frost and protected from chilly winds. It does well in containers with minimal attention— do not fertilize or overwater—and place it in a sunny location that is protected from the cold. French marjoram, a cross with oregano, has a similar taste to sweet marjoram and is much less sensitive to cold, but is not as sweet.

Mint

Mentha spp.

Mint, including peppermint, spearmint and countless other varieties, is a plant with many culinary uses: jelly, sauces, and it makes one of the most refreshing teas on the planet. Mint is easy to grow, but is best confined in containers or parterres because it can be extremely invasive.

Oregano

Origanum vulgare

Oregano is an herb widely used in Italian cookery and a revelation for cooks who have never sampled it fresh from the garden. The dried variety available at most markets is actually a variety of wild Mexican marjoram, with none of the taste of fresh cropped oregano.

Rosemary

Rosmarinus officinalis

Rosemary is another mint that is both a culinary and aromatic herb. It does well in any size container, but a large one planted full of the herb is recommended due to its restorative aroma benefiting the entire garden. Rosemary is not for raised beds because it prefers poor-quality, hardscrabble soil. Purchase rooted stock at a garden centre and plant it in a sunny corner or in a container and, as they say in New

Jersey, forget about it. Rosemary will grow to about 90 cm tall, and when mature it resembles a small pine tree. Rosemary is a tender perennial, and if winters are hard in your locale, simply cut the plant to the base and mulch heavily. If the plant has become artwork it can be dug up, repotted and moved inside to a cool, sunny spot, where it must be misted often. Snip leaves and dry them in a warm, airy, dark place. For culinary purposes, and there are many, the needle-like leaves must be chopped very fine or ground in a pepper grinder.

Sage

Salvia officinalis

This herb loves raised bed cultivation and will grow to over 50 cm tall and become an attractive shrub, but unless the gardener is in the business of manufacturing turkey stuffing, a container is the place for this guy. Plant seeds inside before the last frost or outside after the danger has passed, and keep misting until sprouted. Germination is around 12 days, then thin to 13 cm spacing. If planting from seed, some patience is required because sage takes a while to get established. Once established, sage is very hardy and needs minimal attention. It prefers to be on the dry side, even in summer heat, so exclude the plant from group waterings. When needed for turkey stuffing or wonderful egg dishes, just snip and dry on a sunny windowsill.

Savory

Satureja montana

There are two varieties, winter and summer, with winter savory being the more aromatic. Seeds germinate in 8–10 days, with optimum development reached in 45 days. Winter savory does well in containers and will grow to about 35 cm tall and become an attractive shrub sporting white and mauve flowers. If you want a bigger shrub, summer savory will grow to 45 cm tall and put on a fantastic show with flowers that could be any colour. Either variety will perfume patios and decks and become a topic of conversation. Both varieties are hardy and need minimal care. To harvest, simply cut as needed, and if a lot is needed, cut 20 cm off the top. To dry savory, spread leaves on a screen and let them sit in a dry, shaded area for several days.

Thyme

Thymus vulgaris

Thyme is another aromatic mint widely used to flavour meats and sauces. Thyme does extremely well in rock gardens and other hard-to-grow places and makes a nifty ground cover.

Other Popular Herbs

Coriander/Cilantro

Coriandrum sativum

The seeds are known as coriander, and the leaves are known as cilantro. This plant does not transplant well, so plant seeds early in a container and protect seedlings from frost with a cut plastic bottle. Allow plenty of space, minimum 20 cm, because the plant grows to over 60 cm tall. Coriander has all manner of culinary uses; leaves harvested before flowering (cilantro) are famous for flavouring foods, while seeds harvested from mature plants are used as a spice in baking.

Dill

Anethum graveolens

Dill does not transplant easily, but it is easy to grow from seed. Plant it in either beds or pots, but allow plenty of space, a minimum of 20 cm, because it grows to a fair size. Plant seeds successively biweekly for an all-season crop. If growing dill for seeds, do not plant it near fennel because they will cross-pollinate, making the seeds useless for culinary purposes. If only leaves are required, gardeners may extend the life of the plant by removing the flower heads before they fully develop.

Tarragon

Artemisia dracunculus

Tarragon is one of the few herbs that tolerates partial shade. It is not for raised beds, as the plants prefer to grow in hardscrabble or poor-quality soil. Gardeners are advised to purchase rooted stock at a garden centre or plant nursery. Tarragon requires about 30 cm of space, and once in the ground or container it can be almost forgotten about, as it requires minimal attention. Tarragon will grow to a height of 60 cm and supply cooks with leaves aplenty—snip, air dry in a shady place, and use to flavour vinegar, soups, fish and chicken.

Fruits and Flowers

Micro-orchards

Plants especially bred for small size are called dwarfs, and the even smaller varieties are called miniatures. Dwarf and miniature fruit tree varieties make micro-orchards a possibility almost anywhere in Canada.

Another space-saving technique for fruit growers is to purchase espalier varieties. Espalier is the training of certain fruit trees to grow flat against a trellis or a sun-kissed wall using a pruning method called double horizontal cordon, which is simply allowing only a limited number of horizontal limbs to grow from a strong central leader. It's not a difficult process, and the aesthetic pizzazz it adds to bare walls is astounding, but it does take a few years. Detailed instructions for the espalier training of fruit trees are available in books from your local library or from online sources.

This espalier crabapple takes up much less space than a standard crabapple would.

Bananas

Musa acuminata

Bananas do well in containers and have become popular deck plants in lower BC, with many dinner parties featuring desserts from in-house plantations. But gardeners almost anywhere in the country can manage a crop of scrumptious, pesticide-free bananas if the plant material purchased is several months along. It will take about nine months before partygoers can feast on ripe fruit, so mature plants are recommended, as they will not tolerate a fall frost. Put their containers on wheels, and if cold weather threatens, get them to a warm spot immediately. Plant banana trees in raised bed soil with extra compost added, water often, fertilize with liquid organics once a week, and if growing multiples, keep them close together because their leaves hold onto humid air. After the banana bunch is harvested, the stem dies, but a look at the base will reveal suckers for next season's crop if kept viable during winter.

Citrus

Citrus **spp.**

Gardeners wanting either dwarf or miniature varieties of almost any citrus plant simply have to source the plant locally or order from online plant nurseries, pop them into a proper size container with the correct soil mix and roll them into the sunshine. Most of the quality dwarfed citrus sold in Canada is grown by Monrovia Nurseries in Azusa, California, and comes along with instructions. Gardeners can order direct from Monrovia through their online catalogue, but be warned they charge $30 for the customs paperwork, so a multiple order is wise, as one customs form charge covers all. Oh, and while the citrus trees are tiny, their fruits are regular size, with some bearing fruit soon after repotting. During winter, simply roll them inside to a sunny spot, cut down on water, hold off fertilizing, and come spring it's back to farming citrus.

Figs

Ficus carica

Growing figs has always been a mania with Canadians of Italian or Portuguese descent. Potted plants are available at

almost all garden centres in various stages of growth and variety. Transplant potted plants to a large container with soil that is equal amounts potting soil, aged manure and compost, with some added perlite for drainage. Drainage is vital for figs, so make sure to drill extra holes in the container. If the plant is root-bound when you buy it, and it usually is, transplant as is and then drive a large spike or pointed stick into the soil and root mass; then remove the stick and fill the hole with sand to provide a water channel into the root mass. Water and fertilize often in summer and cut back to almost nothing over winter.

Apples, Peaches, Pears and Plums

Malus spp., *Prunus* spp., *Pyrus* spp.

These trees and others, such as apricot, have all been bred to dwarfism, with some breeders taking it to the max and breeding miniature and columnar trees. The former are no taller than an average person, while columnar trees have very short lateral branches and can only be described as tall and skinny, with regular-sized fruit. As of this writing, only apple trees are available as columnars, but that will soon change. These tree varieties all have different soil and care requirements, so when purchasing them, make sure to get all that pertinent information.

Flower Power

The earth laughs in flowers.

–Ralph Waldo Emerson, poet and lecturer

Flowers are bright and colourful and have the power to cheer anyone up. But their use goes way beyond decorative to downright delicious. The following are some of the most common edible flowers that can be grown by square metre gardeners.

- Borage: the shockingly blue flowers make a marvelous colour contribution to salads.

- Calendula: also known as pot marigolds, they add taste to cooked and uncooked dishes and makes a passable colouring substitute for saffron.

- Herb flowers: allowing a few herbs to flower will provide colour for your garden and salads.

Borage (above); calendula (below)

'Lemon Gem' and 'Orange Gem' marigolds

- Marigolds: both lemon and tangerine gem varieties will impart colour and a citrus flavour to cooked and uncooked dishes, but only the petals are used.

- Naturtiums: these flowers are happiness in the garden and a marvelous trap for aphids; use those that escape aphids in salads and for a vinegar infusion.

- Squash blossoms: great big flowers grow on all varities of squash, and they can be used in culinary preparations.

Gardeners wanting aromatic flowers should plant a few dwarf citrus trees in containers, as they flower profusely, scent the air with divine perfume and bear fruit with unbeatable taste.

Nasturtiums

Conclusion

It is utterly forbidden to be half-hearted about gardening. You have got to love your garden whether you like it or not.

–W.C. Seller and R.J. Yeatman, garden book authors

There is nothing intrinsically difficult about gardening, especially in 3-square-metre beds, it's a simple three-step process—prepare the soil in fall, plant in spring, and harvest crops from late spring to winter. The difficulties arise, as they have for countless generations of gardeners, from constraints, those of water, weeds, weather, insects and time, the latter being the all-encompassing modern day constraint. Intensively planted, 3-square-metre beds will require gardeners to spend time managing the constraints, the water, weeds and insects, none of which are major difficulties if attention or time is allotted to their management. Intensively planted, 3-square-metre raised beds are food factories capable of feeding entire families for the growing season, and like all factories they need management, not constant management, just a steady

hand at the wheel, a daily check to make sure all is well with your charges: check water, check for insects, remove a few bottom leaves, a few errant weeds, clean the bed of any wind-blown debris, tie a few bean, pea, and tomato tendrils, pinch off tomato suckers, check weather forecast, clean and sterilize garden tools, etc. Sounds like work, but it's more like therapy; it heals body and soul and is a mind restorative, or as some forgotten wise man once said, "Gardening is cheaper than therapy, and you get tomatoes."

It's here I get to type the words "the end," and I must confess to being amazed that I am able to do that, since at the start a no-nonsense book about a 3-square-metre pile of soil seemed an impossibility. Suddenly, here's "the end" and no filler required, no pages of tool talk (all gardeners really need is a small shovel), no interminable pages of vegetable varieties (life's an adventure, as is gardening—so close your eyes and pick seed packets because it's going to be good no matter what), and no preaching about raised beds, small, square or otherwise (all gardeners really need is a pile of good soil). This book is basic training in raised bed vegetable gardening. Once read, it will enable seeds to be sown with the greatest expectations of success.

Sources

Arkin, Frieda. *The Essential Kitchen Gardener*. Toronto: Fitzhenry & Whiteside. 1990

Bennett, Jennifer. *The Tomato Handbook*. Toronto: Firefly Publishing. 1997

Billington, Jill. *Really Small Gardens*. London, Eng: Royal Horticultural Society. 1998

Guerra, Michael. *The Edible Container Garden*. New York: Simon & Shuster. 2000

Jabbour, Niki. *Year-Round Vegetable Gardener*. USA: Story Publishing. 2011

Morris, Glenn. *Small Gardens*. New York: Houghton Mifflin. 2002

Morrison, Susan & Sweet, Rebecca. *Garden Up*. USA: Cool Springs Press. 2010

Ruppenthal, R.J. *Fresh Food From Small Spaces*. USA: Chelsea Green Publishing. 2008

Stevens, David. *Small Space Gardens*. New York: Harper Collins. 2003

Staff. *Gardening in Small Spaces*. USA: Taunton Press. 2002

Trail, Gayla. *Grow Great Grub*. New York: Clarkson Potter Publishers. 2010

Yang, Linda. *The City Gardener's Handbook*. USA: Story Books. 1990

Index of Plants

About the Author

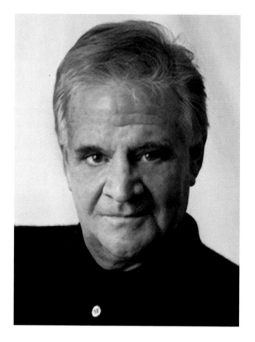

Alan H. Jackson has searched remote jungles for new orchid species, raised bananas in Ecuador, pioneered vanilla beans in New Guinea and introduced Canadians to the tropical delights of passion fruit, guava and cherimoya. Born into a family of food processors, he experienced the food business from harvest to table and witnessed the events that transformed Canadian agriculture from free market enterprise to conglomerate ownership. Weather and gardens are intrinsic to food production and Alan writes on those subjects, drawing on his experiences as a commercial pilot and owner-operator of a large greenhouse/garden centre. Alan attended the University of Guelph, Leicester College and Clark University, and resides in Toronto with his wife, M.